Nineteenth-Century America

COMPLETE ORIGINAL SHEET MUSIC FOR

64 Songs

SELECTED, WITH AN INTRODUCTION AND NOTES, BY

RICHARD JACKSON

HEAD, AMERICANA COLLECTION,
MUSIC DIVISION, NEW YORK PUBLIC LIBRARY

DOVER PUBLICATIONS, INC., NEW YORK

ACKNOWLEDGMENTS

The songs in this volume have been reproduced from very rare original sheet music, nearly all from the fabulous personal collection of Mr. William Lloyd Keepers. The publisher is also grateful to the eminent collector Mr. Lester S. Levy, to the New York Public Library and to the William L. Clements Library of The University of Michigan for making certain items available.

Published in Canada by General Publishing Company, Ltd., 30 Lesmill Road, Don Mills, Toronto, Ontario.
Published in the United Kingdom by Constable and Company, Ltd., 10 Orange Street, London WC 2.

Popular Songs of Nineteenth-Century America: Complete Original Sheet Music for 64 Songs is a new work, first published by Dover Publications, Inc., in 1976.

International Standard Book Number: 0-486-23270-0
Library of Congress Catalog Card Number: 75-30177

Manufactured in the United States of America
Dover Publications, Inc.
180 Varick Street, New York, N.Y. 10014

Introduction

"There's always a reason why something lives."

—George Cukor (from an interview in the television series *The Men Who Made the Movies,* 1973)

I

The consideration of old popular songs can be a fascinating pursuit. And it is a pursuit that can be fascinating on several different levels of consideration. One level has to do with simple (or complex) memory: that faculty of spontaneous recall of people, events and emotions that most of us seem to be blessed (or cursed) with. For those with memories long enough, hearing a song from an older time can trigger a rush of remembrance strong enough sometimes to bring tears to the eyes or cause a nervous tingling along the spine or an involuntary smile or even to activate the senses of taste and smell. This kind of experience can be most pleasurable, certainly nothing to be ashamed of: in fact, it might be thought of as representing a kind of acceptance of one's self and one's past, which can only be a wise thing to do. One writer has described the peculiar nostalgia generated by old songs as the expression "of that pleasant sadness of the days that are no more, so dear to the hearts of youth, the uneducated, the drunken, and nearly every one else, at times" (Hunt, p. 25; see Bibliography).

Occasionally a song comes to have a rather profound personal significance and to a degree that seems in inverse ratio to the actual stuff of the song itself—a simple tune, a scrap of verse. No one, I suppose, really knows why old songs can have such great resonance and the power to stir memories and emotions—not even that old pro Noel Coward seemed to have an answer; in *Private Lives* Amanda can only remark: "Extraordinary how potent cheap music is"—but there is no question that songs can and do have such resonance and power.

Another potentially interesting approach to old songs, one that is more detached and impersonal, is on a historical and cultural level. Not only do the popular songs of another era call to mind certain actual historic events, they can give us important hints as to the preoccupations and ways of thinking of the people who wrote them and the people who bought them and performed them. The use of the term "popular" in regard to music designates, of course, in a broad sense, music intended for or appealing to a mass audience. And since in the popular field the profit motive and the personal ego motive have perhaps always overshadowed the desire for mere "self-expression" or the propagation of ideas or ideals (one could point for example to the statement by Stephen Foster in a famous letter to Edwin P. Christy: "I find I cannot write at all unless I write for public approbation and get credit for what I write"), the producers of popular music attempt to catch the essence—or what they think is the essence—of the public sentiment in their products in hopes of attracting the largest possible segment of the mass audience. The products, then, can perhaps tell us something about the producers as well as the consumers. It is possible, that, apart from the real pleasure they may still hold for us, the chief value of old songs is this glimpse they can afford of a vanished people and a vanished time.

The popular songs of the nineteenth century were created within specific social contexts for a variety of purposes: some were intended for practical use (on the stage, in the church), some to exploit a cause or current event (patriotic songs, war songs) and others simply to entertain (ballads, comic songs). During a large part of the century, the categories were blurred and songs came to serve perhaps several purposes. Songs written for the Sunday School became favorites in the parlor ("Sweet By and By," "Rock of Ages")—this practice followed a fairly established American tradition—and parlor songs found their way to church ("Whispering Hope," "The Little Brown Church"). Songs introduced on the minstrel stage were appropriated as political and military properties ("Dixie," "The Yellow Rose of Texas"). Elegant lavender-scented ballads aimed at the carriage trade became favorite soldier songs ("Lorena"), and one of them ("Aura Lea") was transformed into the dignified graduation song of a prominent military academy. A few songs ("My Old Kentucky Home" and "Carry Me Back to Old Virginny" are two) survived extended exposure to burnt cork and the fumes from innumerable blazing stage gas lamps to become hallowed in another age as official state songs, their gaudy nineteenth-century past forgiven—or at least forgotten.

II

Until the very end of the century, when mechanical pianos with their punched paper rolls, cylinder recordings and finally disc recordings made their appearance in turn, the chief means of disseminating popular music was of course in published form, either as individual pieces of sheet music or as collections. A large measure of the success of a song (or songbook) was judged by the number of copies sold over the counters of retail shops for use in the home, the church, the schoolroom, the lodge or the meeting hall. But for the merchandise to be sold in any volume there first had to be means for *attracting* sales and generating widespread interest, in short: promotion—that pursuit for which America would become famous, but which in the nineteenth century was only in the infant stages of what in the twentieth would be developed into a science and an art (one of the black arts, certainly). For years, one of the basic modes of advertising was the use of published notices in newspapers and journals; for example:

> Just published and for sale, new music—The bird waltz, as a duett. (*New York Evening Post*, February 12, 1824)

> Firth, Pond & Co.
> As specimens of our popular pieces we will mention
> THE OLD FOLKS AT HOME,
> That most beautiful American melody, nearly *Forty Thousand Copies* of which have already been sold! also,
> NELLY BLY,
> That popular Ethiopian melody . . . . (*The Musical World and New York Musical Times*, January 8, 1853)

> Oh! The Old, Old Clock. By J. A. Fowler.
> A most excellent song of the good old style. It can not but be a lasting favorite. The music though not difficult, has that easy self-singing peculiarity that insures popularity. 30¢
> (*Philadelphia Musical Journal*, April 9, 1856)

But this kind of promotion reached only relatively few people. The most important impact on the spread of popular music and the concomitant rise of sheet-music sales was that of the live performance. It was the more-or-less high-powered, more-or-less professional individuals and groups, appearing in recital or theatrical formats, that had the greatest effect on the trade. Individual performers such as Thomas ("Daddy") Rice (1808–1860), one of the earliest Negro stage impersonators, began touring in the 1820s with theatrical troupes and circuses, presenting his famous "Jim Crow" act in songs and skits (the song "Jim Crow," 1828, has been called the first American popular song to gain a great international reputation). Foreign stars such as the Swedish soprano Jenny Lind (1820–1887), brought to the United States in 1850 by P. T. Barnum, and the English singer and songwriter Henry Russell (1812–1900) traveled extensively and helped create a large new market for various kinds of popular music. Russell, in particular, who lived in this country for nine years in the 1830s and '40s, created a sensation with his own skillfully contrived, highly colored melodramatic ballads such as "The Maniac," "The Ship on Fire" and "Woodman! Spare That Tree!" (included in this collection). He made a comfortable income from his performing career, while his numerous songs, which sold in the thousands of copies, made several publishers wealthy.

In the early 1840s there arose an institution that would form another most important adjunct to the commercial music business and that would flourish and survive, in one form or another, until the end of the century: it was, of course, the blackface minstrel show. This amazing native entertainment phenomenon, this raucous mixture of bastard ethnic comedy and music, undoubtedly contributed to the launching of American music publishing on its way to becoming big business. The minstrel troupes, playing for long runs in the cities and touring throughout the country and abroad, needed a steady supply of material for their shows. Composers were eager to provide new songs and publishers eager to bring them out as potential new hits "Performed by the Christy Minstrels" or some other popular group. The large segment of the public that comprised the audience for the minstrel shows over the decades also formed a built-in market for the published songs. This cyclical pattern and the combination of popular entertainment, musical talent and exploitation became a permanent fixture on the American scene. The form of the entertainments gradually changed—the minstrel show gave way to the variety theater, vaudeville, operetta, musical comedy and so on—but the essential elements of the formula remained fairly intact.

Another kind of early musical entertainment that both fed and promoted nineteenth-century publishing was that of the singing families. There were several of these groups that attained considerable fame, performing in the villages and towns of the countryside and also in the big cities. The most prominent and long-lasting of the groups was the Hutchinson Family of New Hampshire, composed originally of three brothers and a sister—John, Asa, Judson and Abby—from a family of thirteen. As the original members married and had children, and other members of the family got into the act, the group split into several "tribes"—the tribe of Asa, of John, etc.—thus forming a multiplicity of performing units. The original quartet began its career in the 1840s, traveling in a wagon around New Hampshire and neighboring states; they took instruments with them—violins, guitar, cello—to accompany their vocal numbers. For almost half a century the Hutchinson Family, in its various tribes, performed most of the best-known popular songs and hymns of the era (including pieces by their friend Henry Russell) and introduced a number of them, such as Kittredge's "Tenting on the Old Camp Ground" (included here). They shrewdly capitalized on most of the fads of the day and were very much involved with the current reform movements—abolition, women's suffrage and temperance—and so promoted these causes with propaganda songs, some of them composed by members of the family. The Oliver Ditson Company of Boston published much of the Hutchinson repertory over the years with considerable success. The audiences that flocked to their concerts in New York and Boston and innumerable small towns from Maine to Minnesota became the customers at the music counters, eager for a stirring or melancholy Hutchinson favorite to play and sing in their own homes.

The greatest single boost of the century to the propagation of popular music and the prosperity of the music publishers was the greatest single event of the century, the four-year cataclysm of the Civil War. Wars are of course always good for business, and this war was as beneficial for the music business as it was for many others. Not only did it create a new market for the kinds of songs associated with wartime, such as marching songs, rallying songs and other patriotic and propagandistic material, it provided abundant subject matter for comic songs, pathetic soldier ballads and songs dealing with home and family. It probably generated more popular music than any other event in the country's history; furthermore, among this cascade of war music were some of the most memorable songs of the century.

The market for the new material was large and apparently omnivorous. The songs were taken up by military and civilian bands; they were sung at rallies and meetings of various kinds and in churches; they were performed in the popular theater and by the singing families; they were used by composers as themes for elaborate piano variations that thrilled audiences in the concert rooms. A considerable number of the public, especially in the North, awaited each new release as they would the latest dispatch in the daily newspaper. The songs undoubtedly helped families around their pianos feel somehow intimately involved in the great struggle, a sense of being part of the grand and terrible events, whether or not they had relatives in the field.

When the war was over so was the boom time of the popular music business. It took years for the publishing houses to regain anything like the prosperity of the war years. To compensate, a number of them began to diversify their activities and went into the manufacture and sale of pianos and organs, which proved to be a highly lucrative pursuit.

III

This collection does not carry with it any claim that the 64 songs included were either *the* most popular in America during the nineteenth century or that they are even fully representative of those most popular.* There were many thousands of pieces for the popular market published during the span of the century (the *Complete Catalogue* of the Board of Music Trade, for example, listed approximately eighty thousand songs and instrumental pieces, most of them of a light or popular nature, published by the twenty publisher-members of the Board and available for purchase as of 1870), and from among these thousands perhaps hundreds (the exact number is impossible to calculate) sold well and attained varying degrees of use and fame. Many of the songs most popular in their day, however, are now, in the last quarter of the twentieth century, totally forgotten by the public at large. Songs of great former prominence that rang from stages and parlors all over the country have fallen into dense obscurity. They do not exist in living memory but only in fugitive sheet-music copies preserved in the larger research libraries and the more comprehensive private collections. They make fascinating reading.

* Not included in this volume are theater songs (other than minstrel numbers) or songs from the last decade of the nineteenth century, since these are already well represented in the following Dover volumes: *Favorite Songs of the Nineties* (ed. Robert A. Fremont), *Song Hits from the Turn of the Century* (eds. Paul Charosh & Robert A. Fremont) and *Show Songs from "The Black Crook" to "The Red Mill"* (ed. Stanley Appelbaum).

But some, actually a relative few, *have* survived, not only in memory but in actual use, and it is with this sturdy minority that we are concerned here. The one modest claim that can be made for this collection is that it presents a cross section of those songs of a former age that have somehow endured and that still enjoy a certain currency.

Why is it that certain songs have survived while others have not? To what can we attribute their unusual longevity? One epigrammatic English writer, S. J. Adair Fitz-Gerald, suggested in the 1890s that "The evolution of the popular song presents a striking illustration of the survival of the unfittest" (Fitz-Gerald, p. 102). This is a clever remark, but it is also a foolish remark by a critic who made the mistake of attempting to evaluate popular music with the tools of High Culture. He further exposed his unfortunate bias in remarks directed specifically at American songs: "Minor songs of a more or less negro [*sic*] blend have been turned out in thousands, and have grown into favour with the general public of most nations. But as yet only the 'Star-Spangled Banner,' 'Columbia the Gem of the Ocean,' 'Hail, Columbia,' and 'America' have appeared as national productions, neither of which is in any way admirable" (Fitz-Gerald, p. 96). Here the critic casually dismisses (in rather curious grammar) four of the most cherished and widely used American songs, and he finds nothing at all remarkable in the fact that, by his own estimate, thousands of other American songs have become popular *with the general public of most nations.*

Popular songs do not attain true popularity, do not survive—nor do they perish—because they possess superior artistic qualities. To be sure, many songs in this collection do have genuinely fine "artistic" touches—there a fine assertive tune or perhaps a gracefully arched melodic line, there a deft harmonic progression, there a stroke of vivid textual imagery—but it is not these qualities in particular that have kept them alive. For there are also songs here that seem in no way extraordinary (except maybe in negative ways: what we might now consider the heavy-handed sentimentality of many, for instance). We may wonder at the measure of affection and delight they once sustained and—in certain instances—still do. We perhaps strain to see them through the eyes of another century to discover the secret of their strength. No, the "good" and the "bad" alike have survived.

One test that finally obliterates any serious consideration of Mr. Fitz-Gerald's Darwinian-theory-in-reverse, and one that would totally confuse our English friend, is the test of wide comparison. To examine a large quantity of forgotten nineteenth-century songs and compare them, say, with the select contemporaneous group in this collection is to discover that there is frequently little apparent difference between those now unknown and those still famous. For every one that somehow survived, one finds dozens, hundreds, that seem cut from the very same cloth; and those hundreds appear to suffer no striking qualitative disadvantages in tune or text to the special few.

IV

Certain songs, through the circumstances and dimension of their initial popularity, achieved and maintained so secure a niche in their own time that they have been written about and discussed as cultural artifacts, a kind of antique Pop Art, as it were. This is one rather circumscribed way in which they have remained in our consciousness. Then, too, many of these same songs have been printed in different arrangements in widely used anthologies such as community songbooks, college songbooks, Boy Scout songbooks, etc., thus insuring perpetual revival.

A few songs have become so strongly associated with an occasion that perhaps no one alive can remember the origins of that association. "Jingle Bells," for example, has for so long been part of the Christmas celebration that it seems timeless, its origins lost in some dim folk past. Many people who have loved it, accepted it or merely endured it as part of their lives might be surprised to learn that it began its career as just one of many ordinary, fairly pleasant pieces vying for commercial success in the marketplace of the late 1850s.

Certain songs, after totally casual and inauspicious beginnings, were transformed by events and came to have great meaning for later generations, far greater meaning, occasionally, than for the generation that first knew the song. I am thinking, for instance, of a song that apparently started life in embryonic form within the measures of an obscure Methodist hymn ("Say, Brothers, Will You Meet Us"); at the beginning of the Civil War it was taken up and changed by anonymous hands for use with new words as a soldier song; it was further anonymously altered for other words, and the phrases "John Brown's Body" and "Glory, Hallelujah" entered the language; it was published in several versions; still later a Northern intellectual and writer composed a set of fairly austere, vaguely religious verses that matched the tune and the whole was again published as "Battle Hymn of the Republic." This song, with its checkered, not especially noble, history has come to have layers of significance, both historical and personal, for the generations that followed. At a point in time far removed from the advent of this song, many would find it all but impossible to think of it purely in the light of its original meanings and use. Many associate it, broadly, with the Civil War and the reunification of the country. Many associate it somehow with Lincoln. Others regard it, indistinctly, as some kind of patriotic number suitable for school children or Kate Smith. Yet others, of a younger twentieth-century generation, may have it identified with the funeral of Robert Kennedy, thus giving it a whole new set of potential associations. Other songs with quite different histories have come to assume positions similar to the "Battle Hymn": "America," "Dixie" and many songs by Stephen Foster, for instance, have assumed special meanings and varying degrees of importance in our lives.

Some old songs are kept current simply because they have been appropriated and reworked for commercial purposes, and they frequently enjoy new popularity. "When You and I Were Young Maggie Blues" (1922), "Love Me Tender" (1956)—based on "Aura Lea" (1861)—and"Jingle Bell Rock" (1957) are three adaptations that come immediately to mind.

It is perhaps almost too obvious a point to require stating that the factor of use is actually one of the most important in sustaining the life of a song, for assuring its existence as part of the fabric of our everyday lives. How else, really, would the transient aural creations of another century, especially popular creations that are by usual definition ephemeral, remain in our ears if indeed they were not performed? A great many *are* performed, though we may be aware of their presence only in a somewhat subliminal way. A major medium by which these fragile though curiously durable melodies are communicated is that marvelous child of the twentieth century, the motion picture—especially the motion picture in its television habitat. The magic box in the home has become the repository of virtually the entire history of American sound movies, and it is available to millions, in installments, every day and night. The classic films, the grade-Z potboilers, the costume spectacles, the musicals, the comedies and dramas—they are all there in seemingly unending parade.

For years film composers have used popular tunes from the nineteenth century in their background scores. Men such as Max Steiner (1888–1971), Dimitri Tiomkin (b. 1894), Elmer Bernstein (b. 1922) and Aaron Copland (b. 1900, known mainly as a composer of concert music, who made such effective use of the song "Plaisir d'amour" in his score for *The Heiress*, 1949) have been especially astute in finding songs relevant to specific periods and weaving them into their music. They have used this technique most often in historical pictures and westerns. Steiner's classic score for *Gone With the Wind* (1939) probably holds the record for use of nineteenth-century tunes as thematic material; quoted in snatches and in fairly extended passages are Foster's "Camptown Races," "Dolly Day," "Lou'siana Belle," "Massa's in de Cold Ground," "My Old Kentucky Home" "Katie Bell," "Old Black Joe," "Old Folks at Home," "Ring de Banjo" and "Under the Willow She's Sleeping," as well as Root's "Tramp! Tramp! Tramp!," Work's "Marching Through Georgia," Emmett's "Dixie" and "The Bonnie Blue Flag" and "Maryland, My Maryland!" Here Steiner not only capitalized superbly on the general familiarity of the pieces to help sustain a feeling of time and place, he incidentally assured the survival of these pieces in a vivid aural experience for as long as *Gone With the Wind* is shown.

Certain directors seem to favor the use of old songs in their pictures. John Ford (1895–1973), for example, must have worked closely with the composers on his pictures. He apparently had a roster of favorite pieces that appear with regularity throughout his work, and chief among the favorites seems to be Lowry's "Beautiful River" ("Shall We Gather at the River").

Old songs also appear unpredictably in "modern" film comedies and melodramas, i.e. stories set more or less at the time of the film's making. Two examples: "The Flying Trapeze," featured in a prominent group-sing sequence in *It Happened One Night* (1934), and "Beautiful Dreamer," used to comic and ironic effect in *Mighty Joe Young* (1949) to pacify the giant gorilla who is the film's star. ("Beautiful Dreamer" served in a very different capacity as a leitmotif for the character of the mother played by Lillian Gish in *Duel in the Sun,* 1946.)

Occasionally in films, a nineteenth-century song is used within a certain context that gives it a new twist of meaning to twentieth-century minds. In *The Battle of San Pietro* (1944), John Huston's superb documentary film of the Italian campaign in World War II, we see Italian villagers digging graves for American soldiers killed in the battle. On the sound track at this moment we hear the strains of George Allen's "The Ocean Burial" (1850) which is familiar to us largely in its frontier version, "Oh, Bury Me Not on the Lone Prairie." The sound of this tune, with its multiple associations, in conjunction with the images on the screen creates a new poignancy and a sudden terrible awareness: the mind's eye encompasses all the battlefields of that war and the lonely graves of Americans on foreign soil. One must stop and realize that much of the effect of this powerful sequence stems from the use of a genteel parlor song written in 1850. This realization can come as something of a culture shock.

Movies constantly remind us of music from the past: what it was; what it means; why it lives. Much as minstrel shows and the other forms of live public musicmaking served so importantly to introduce and to disseminate the music of the nineteenth century to contemporary generations, movies may prove to be the most significant instrument for performing similar functions for this music with later generations.

New York City
January 1975

RICHARD JACKSON

Contents

The songs are arranged in alphabetical order (not counting "A" or "The" at the beginning of a title). Well-known alternate titles are cross-referenced (e.g., "The Blue Tail Fly: *see* Jim Crack Corn"). Anonymous and spurious authors of words and music are not listed. The publishers given are those of the editions being reprinted; the dates, those that appear on the music sheets. For further information on authorship, dating, original publishers and the like, see the Notes on the Music, beginning on page 261.

ADESTE FIDELES

The favorite PORTUGUEZ HYMN On the NATIVITY.

Deum de DEO lumen de lumine,
Gestant puella viscere
Deum verum genitum non factum,
Venite adoremus Dominum

Cantet nunc Io. chorus angelorum,
Cantet nunc aula cœlustium,

Ergo qui natus die hodierna,
JESU tibi sit gloria,
Patris æterni verbum caro factum;
Venite adoremus Dominumm

Gloria in excelsis DEO,
Venite adoremus Dominum

W.P.

ALL QUIET

ALONG THE

POTOMAC

TO-NIGHT.

BALTIMORE: 3.

Published by MILLER & BEACHAM, No. 10 North Charles Street.

"ALL QUIET ALONG THE POTOMAC TO-NIGHT."

noth-ing! a pri-vate or two now and then, Will not count in the news of the bat-tle, Not an
of-fi-cer lost! on-ly one of the men Moaning out all a-lone the death rattle. "All
qui-et a-long...... the Po-to-mac to-night!"
f

2

"All quiet along the Potomac to-night,"
Where the soldiers lie peacefully dreaming,
And their tents in the rays of the clear autumn moon,
And the light of the camp fires are gleaming;
There's only the sound of the lone sentry's tread,
As he tramps from the rock to the fountain,
And thinks of the two on the low trundle bed
Far away in the cot on the mountain.

3

His musket falls slack_ his face, dark and grim,
Grows gentle with memories tender,
As he mutters a pray'r for the children asleep,
And their mother_"May heaven defend her!"
The moon seems to shine as brightly as then_
That night, when the love yet unspoken
Leap'd up to his lips, and when low murmur'd vows
Were pledg'd, to be ever unbroken.

4

Then drawing his sleeve roughly o'er his eyes,
He dashes off the tears that are welling,
And gathers his gun close up to his breast,
As if to keep down the heart's swelling;
He passes the fountain, the blasted pine tree,
And his footstep is lagging and weary,
Yet onward he goes, thro' the broad belt of light,
Toward the shades of the forest so dreary.

5

Hark! was it the night-wind that rustles the leaves!
Was it the moonlight so wond'rously flashing?
It look'd like a rifle! "Ha, Mary good bye!"
And his life-blood is ebbing and plashing.
"All quiet along the Potomac to-night,"
No sound save the rush of the river;
While soft falls the dew on the face of the dead,
"The Picket's" off duty for ever.

Clayton.

OUR COUNTRY'S SONGS

Star Spangled Banner.	Yankee Doodle.
Hail Columbia.	Red, White & Blue.
Stand by the Flag.	Vive l'America.
Columbia rules the sea.	Unfurl the glorious Banner.
Our Union right or wrong.	America.

ALBANY. J. H. HIDLEY. NEW YORK. PUBLISHED BY FIRTH, POND & Co. 547 BROADWAY. CINCINNATI C. Y. FONDA.

AMERICA,

MY COUNTRY 'TIS OF THEE.

SONG AND CHORUS

ARRANGED BY HENRY TUCKER.

My coun - try! 'tis of thee, Sweet land of li - ber - ty,

Of thee I sing; Land where my fa - ther's died, Land of the

pil - grims pride, From eve - ry moun - tain side Let free - dom ring.

CHORUS.
AIR.
ALTO.
TENOR.
BASS.
PIANO.
1 Land where my fa - ther's died, Land of the Pil - grims pride,
2 I love thy rocks and rills, Thy woods and tem - pled hills:
3 Let mor - tal tongues a - wake; Let all that breathe par - take;
1 Land where my fa - ther's died, Land of the Pil - grims pride,
4 Long may our land be bright With free - dom's ho - ly light;
From ev - ry moun - tain side Let Free - dom ring.
My heart with rap - ture thrills, Like that a - bove.
Let rocks their si - lence break The sound pro - long.
From ev - ry moun - tain side Let Free - dom ring.
Pro - tect us by thy might, Great God, our King!

tem - pled hills: My heart with rap - ture thrills, Like that a - bove.
breathe par - take; Let rocks their si - lence break, The sound pro - long.
ho - ly light; Pro - tect us by thy might, Great God, our King!

THE

ARKANSAS TRAVELLER

BY

MOSE CASE.

BOSTON.

Published by Oliver Ditson & Co. 277 Washington St.

Cin.	N. York.	Boston.	Phil^a
J. Church Jr.	W. A. Pond & Co.	J. C. Haynes & Co.	J. E. Gould.

Dwn & Engd by H. F. Greene.

THE ARKANSAS TRAVELLER.

This piece is intended to represent an Eastern man's experience among the inhabitants of Arkansas, showing their hospitality and the mode of obtaining it.

Several years since he was travelling the State to Little Rock, the Capitol;— in those days Rail Roads had not been heard of and the Stage lines were very limited, so under the circumstances, he was obliged to travel the whole distance on foot. One evening about dusk he came across a small log house standing fifteen or twenty yards from the road and enclosed by a low rail fence, of the most primitive description. In the door sat a man playing a Violin; the tune was the "Arkansas Traveller," then, the most popular tune in that region. He kept repeating the first part of the tune over and over again, as he could not play the second part. At the time the traveller reached the house it was raining very hard, and he was anxious to obtain shelter from the storm; — the house looked anything but a shelter, as it was covered with clapboards and the rain was leaking into every part of it. The old man's daughter Sarah appeared to be getting supper, while a small boy was setting the table, and the old lady sat in the door near her husband, admiring the music.
The Stranger on coming up, said: —"How do you do?" — the man merely glanced at him and continuing to play, said: —"I do as I please."

Stranger. — How long have you been living here?
Old Man. — D'ye see that mountain there? — Well, that was there when I come here.
S. — Can I stay here tonight?
O.M. — No! ye can't stay here.

S. — How long will it take me to get to the next Tavern?
O.M. — Well, you'll not get thar at all if you stand thar foolin with me all night.
(Plays.)

S. — Well, how far do you call it to the next Tavern?

O.M. — I reckon its upwards of some distance.

S. — I am very dry, do you keep any spirits in your house?

O.M. — Do you think my house is haunted? they say there's plenty down in the Grave-yard.

S. — How do they cross this river ahead? *O.M.* — The ducks all swim across.

S. — How far is it to the forks of the road?

O.M. — I've been living here nigh on twenty years and no road aint forked yit.

S. — Give me some satisfaction if you please sir; where does this road go to?

O.M. — Well, it hain't moved a step since I've been here.

S. — Why don't you cover your house? it leaks; *O.M.* — Cause its raining.

S. — Then why don't you cover it when its not raining? *O.M.* — Cause it don't leak.

S. — Why don't you play the second part of that tune?

O.M. — If you're a better player than I am you can play it yourself. I'll bring the Fiddle out to you, I don't want you in here.

(Stranger plays the second part of the tune.)

O. M. — Git over the fence and come in and sit down, I didn't know you could play. You can board here if you want to — kick that dog off that stool and set down and play it over, I want to hear it again.

(Stranger plays second part again.)

O.M. — Our supper is ready now, won't you have some with us? *S.* — If you please!
O.M. — What will you take, Tea or Coffee? *S.* — A cup of Tea if you please!
O.M. — Sall, git the grubbin hoe and go dig some sassafras, quick!

(Old Man plays the first part.)

S. — (To the little Boy.) Bub give me a knife and fork if you please.
Boy. — We haint got no knives and forks sir. *S.* — Then give me a spoon. *B.* — We haint got no spoons neither. *S.* — Well then, how do you do? *B.* — Tolerable, thank you, how do you do sir?

The Stranger finding such poor accommodations, and thinking his condition could be bettered by leaving, soon left and finally succeeded in finding a Tavern with better fare. He has never had the courage to visit Arkansas since.

TO

S.C. Campbell. Esq.

OF HOOLEY & CAMPBELL'S MINSTRELS.

AURA LEA

SONG & CHORUS

Poetry by

W. W. FOSDICK ESQ.

Music by

GEO. R. POULTON.

CINCINNATI

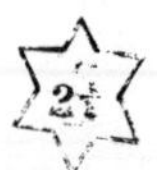

Published by J. CHURCH Jr. 66 West 4th St

NEW YORK. Firth Pond & Co. | BOSTON. O. Ditson & Co. | N. ORLEANS. P. P. Werlein

2½

T. I. Frost.

AURA LEA.

mf
SONG.
PIANO.
p
When the Blackbird in the Spring, On the wil-low-tree Sat and rock'd, I
heard him sing, Singing Au-ra Lea. Au-ra Lea, Au-ra Lea, Maid of golden
cres
hair; Sunshine came a-long with thee, And swallows in the air.
CHORUS.V.S.

CHORUS.
1st time Forte, 2nd time Piano.
TREBLE.
Au - ra Lea......, Maid of gold - - en hair;
ALTO.
Au - ra Lea, Maid of gold - - en hair;
TENOR.
Au - ra Lea..............................of gold - en hair;
BASS.
PIANO.
dim.
Sunshine came a - long with thee, And swallows in the air.
dim.
Sunshine came a - long with thee, And swallows in the air.
dim.
Sunshine came a - long with thee, And swallows in the air.
dim.
Sunshine came a - long with thee, And swallows in the air.
dim.

SECOND VERSE.

In thy blush the rose was born,
 Music, when you spake,
Through thine azure eye the morn,
 Sparkling, seemed to break.
Aura Lea, Aura Lea,
 Birds of crimson wing
Never song have sung to me
 As in that sweet spring.
CHORUS. Aura Lea, Aura Lea,
 Maid of golden hair;
 Sunshine came along with thee,
 And swallows in the air.

THIRD VERSE.

Aura Lea! the bird may flee,
 The willow's golden hair
Swing through winter fitfully,
 On the stormy air.
Yet if thy blue eyes I see,
 Gloom will soon depart;
For to me, sweet Aura Lea
 Is sunshine through the heart.
CHORUS. Aura Lea, &c.

FOURTH VERSE.

When the mistletoe was green,
 Midst the winter's snows,
Sunshine in thy face was seen,
 Kissing lips of rose.
Aura Lea, Aura Lea,
 Take my golden ring;
Love and light return with thee,
 And swallows with the spring.
CHORUS. Aura Lea, &c.

THE

The Battle-Cry of Freedom.

Words & Music by

GEO. F. ROOT.

Publised by ROOT & CADY 95 Clark St.
CHICAGO.

S. BRAINARD & CO.—CLEVELAND. H. TOLMAN & CO.—BOSTON H. N. HEMPSTED—MILWAUKEE

THE

BATTLE CRY OF FREEDOM.

GEO. F. ROOT.

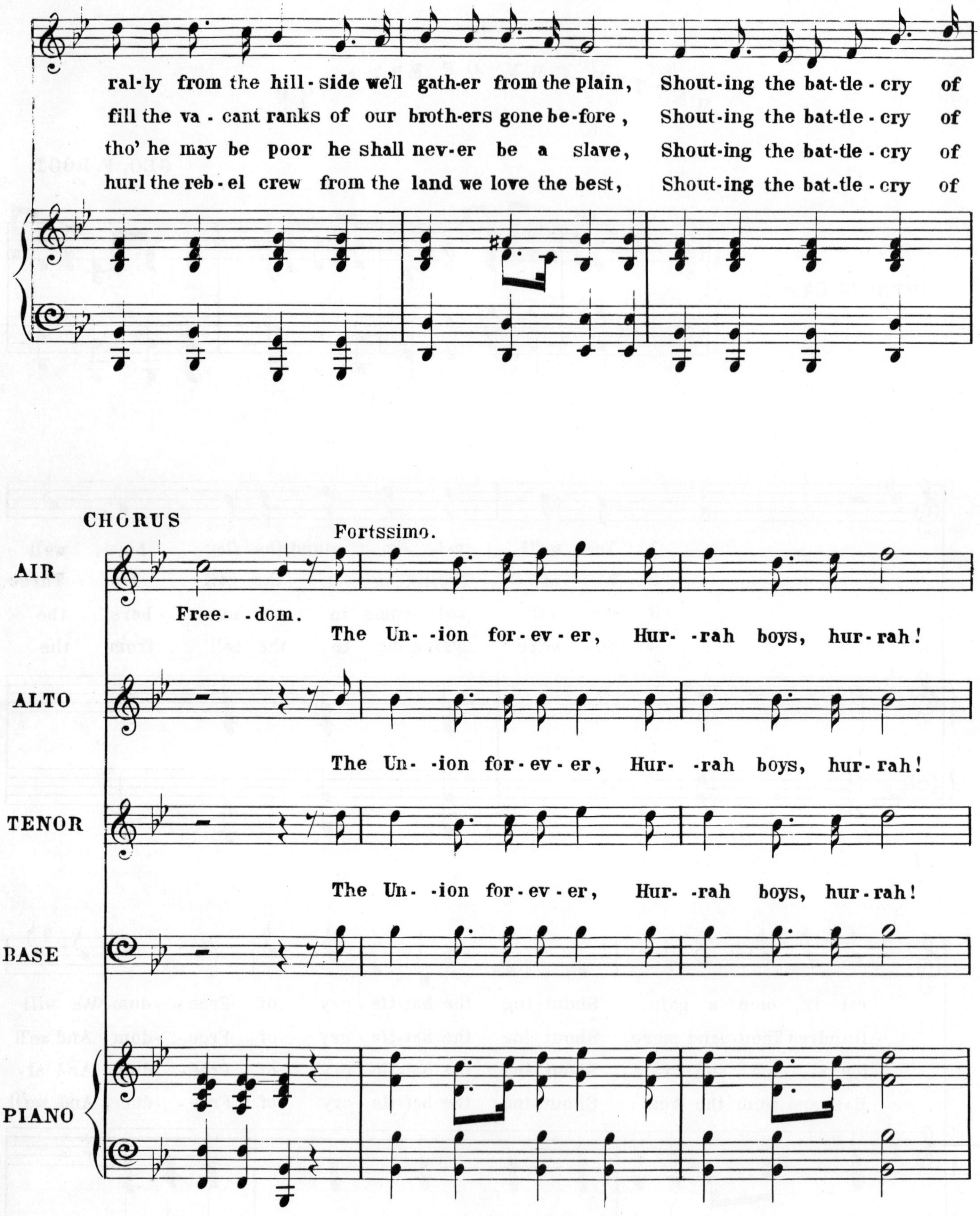

CHORUS

Fortssimo.

AIR

Free- -dom.

The Un-ion for-ev-er, Hur- -rah boys, hur-rah!

ALTO

The Un- -ion for-ev-er, Hur- -rah boys, hur-rah!

TENOR

The Un- -ion for-ev-er, Hur- -rah boys, hur-rah!

BASE

PIANO

Down with the Trai-tor, Up with the Star; While we ral-ly round the flag, boys,
Down with the Trai-tor, Up with the Star; While we ral-ly round the flag, boys,
Down with the Trai-tor, Up with the Star; While we ral-ly round the flag, boys,
Ral-ly once a--gain, Shout-ing the bat-tle--cry of Free- -dom.
Ral-ly once a-gain, Shout-ing the bat-tle--cry of Free- -dom.
Ral-ly once a-gain, Shout-ing the bat-tle--cry of Free- -dom.

"Glory, Hallelujah,"

WRITTEN BY

Mrs. Dr. S. G. Howe,

FOR THE

ATLANTIC MONTHLY.

BOSTON.
Published by Oliver Ditson & Co. 277 Washington St.

Firth Pond & Co.	J. Church Jr.	J. C. Haynes & Co.	J. E. Gould	C. C. Clapp & Co.
N. York.	Cin.	Boston	Philada	Boston.

BATTLE HYMN OF THE REPUBLIC.

CHORUS.

Glo - ry! Glo-ry Hal-le-lu - - jah! Glo-ry! Glory! Glory Halle - lu - jah!
Glo - ry! Glo-ry Hal-le-lu - jah! Glo-ry!Glory! Glory Halle - lu - jah!
Glo - ry! Glo-ry Hal-le-lu - jah! Glo-ry!Glory! Glory Halle - lu - jah!

Glo - ry! Glo-ry Hal-le - lu - jah! His truth is marching on.
Glo - ry! Glo-ry Hal-le - lu - jah! His truth is marching on.
Glo - ry! Glo-ry Hal-le - lu - jah! His truth is marching on.

2. I have seen Him in the watch-fires of a hundred circling camps, They have
3. I have read a fie - ry gos - pel writ in burnished rows of steel: "As ye
4. He has sounded forth the trumpet that shall nev - er call retreat; He is
5. In the beauty of the lil - lies Christ was born across the sea, With a
builded Him an al - tar in the evening dews and damps; I can read His righteous sentence by the
deal with my contemners, so with you my grace shall deal; Let the He - ro born of wo - man crush the
sift - ing out the hearts of men be - fore His judgment seat: Oh, be swift, my soul, to answer Him! be
glo - ry in his bo - som that trans - fig - ures you and me: As he died to make men ho - ly, let us
dim and flaring lamps: His day is march - ing on.
ser - pent with his heel, Since God is march - ing on.
ju - bi - lant, my feet! Our God is march - ing on.
die to make men free, While God is march ing on.
Chorus.
Chorus.

BY REV. R. LOWRY

ARRANGED FOR PIANOFORTE OR MELODEON

BY

E. MACK

This beautiful composition is issued by permission of the "American Tract Society of N.Y." and is taken from their popular Sabbath School book "Happy Voices."

Holmes & Gordon, Engrs. Phila.

3

Published by W. R. SMITH AGT. 135 N.th 8th St.

New York W. A. Pond & Co | Harrisburg H. C. Orth | Boston O. Ditson & Co | Erie Pa Weigle & Zeigler | Pittsburgh Wamelink & Barr | Cleveland S. Brainard & Sons | A. C. Peters & Bro

BEAUTIFUL RIVER.

MUSIC BY REV: R. LOWRY. ARRANGED BY E. MACK.

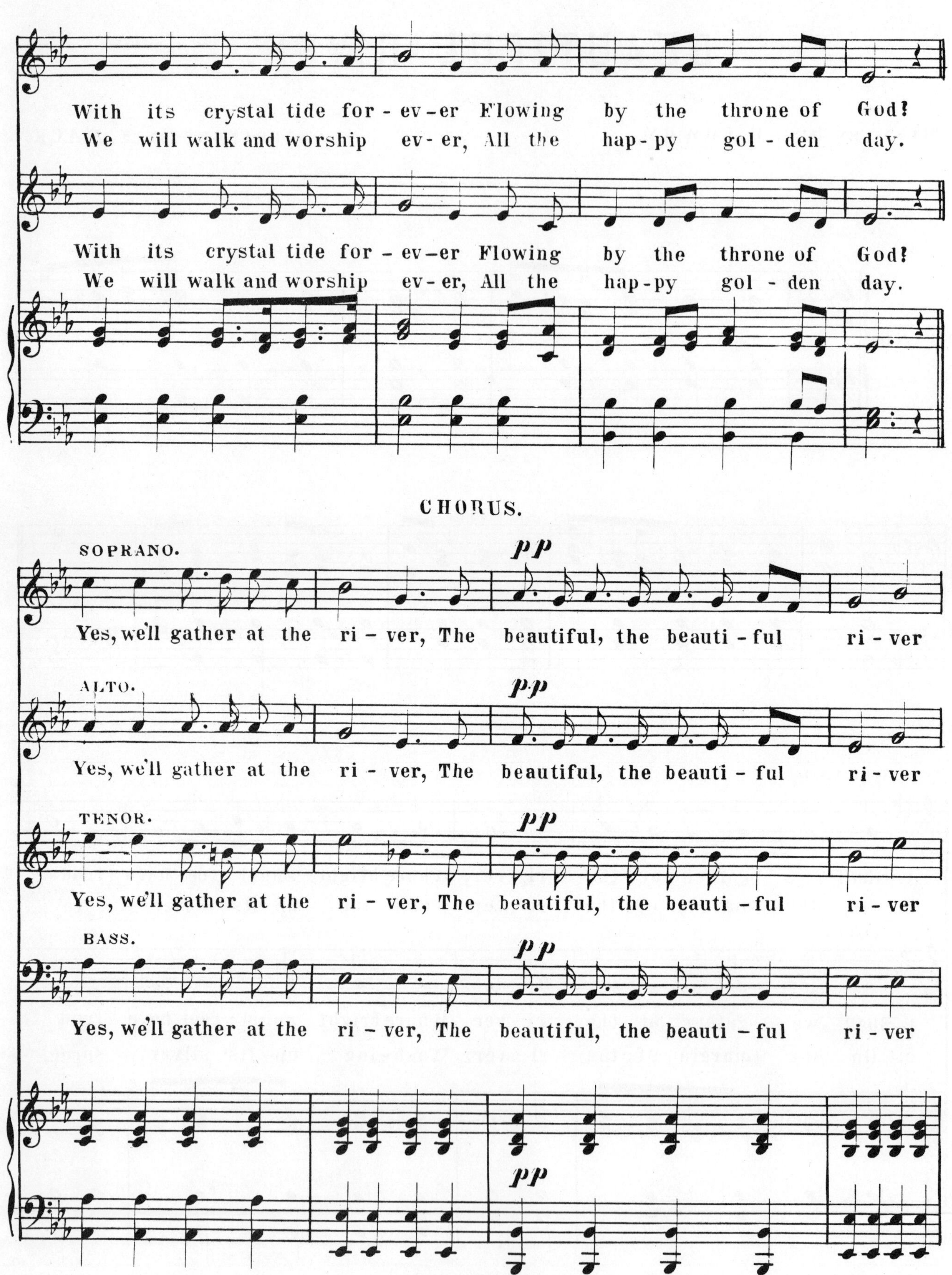
With its crystal tide for - ev - er Flowing by the throne of God!
We will walk and worship ev - er, All the hap - py gol - den day.
With its crystal tide for - ev - er Flowing by the throne of God!
We will walk and worship ev - er, All the hap - py gol - den day.
CHORUS.
SOPRANO.
pp
Yes, we'll gather at the ri - ver, The beautiful, the beauti - ful ri - ver
ALTO.
pp
Yes, we'll gather at the ri - ver, The beautiful, the beauti - ful ri - ver
TENOR.
pp
Yes, we'll gather at the ri - ver, The beautiful, the beauti - ful ri - ver
BASS.
pp
Yes, we'll gather at the ri - ver, The beautiful, the beauti - ful ri - ver
pp

3.

On the bosom of the river,
Where our Saviour-king we own,
We shall meet,and sorrow never
'Neath the glory of the throne.

Chorus.

4.

Ere we reach the shining river,
Lay we every burden down,
Grace our spirits will deliver
And provide a robe and crown.

Chorus.

5.

At the smiling of the river,
Mirror of the Savior's face,
Saints whom death will never sever,
Lift their songs of saving grace.

Chorus.

6.

Soon we'll reach the silver river,
Soon our pilgrimage will cease;
Soon our happy hearts will quiver
With the melody of peace.

Chorus.

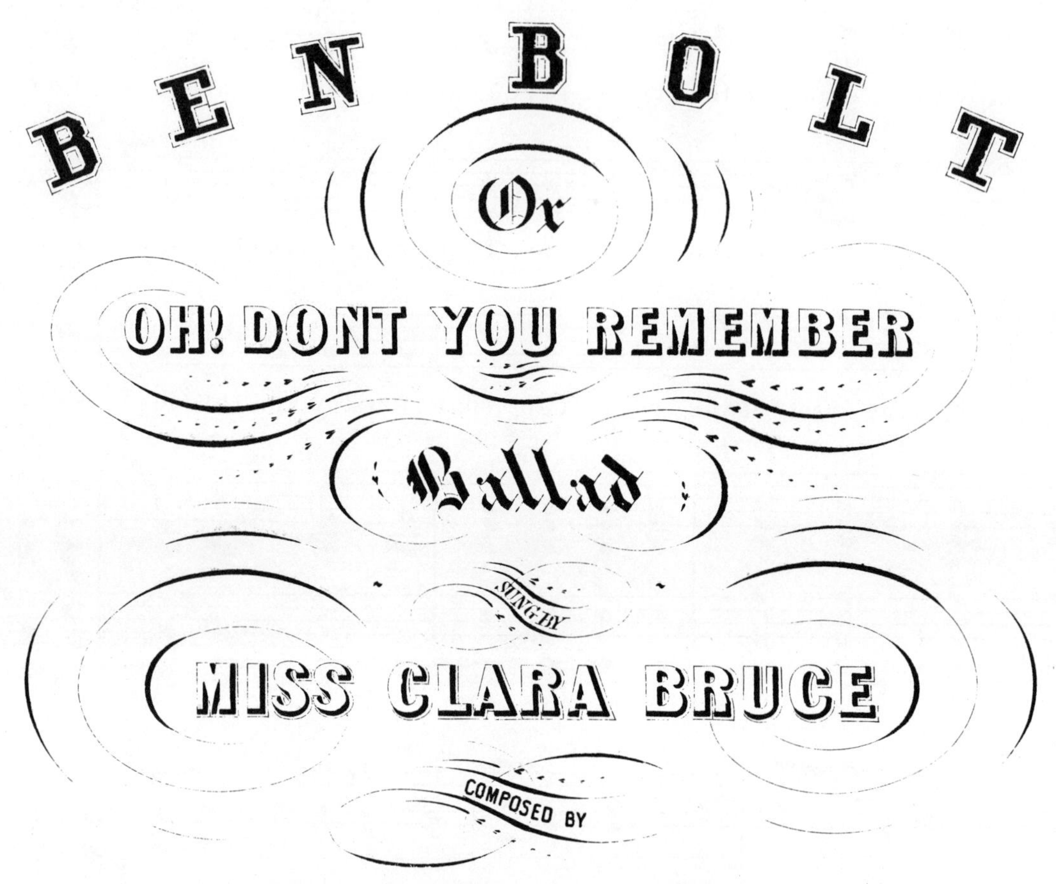

NELSON KNEASS.

Piano Accomp. 25 Cts. nett. Guitar Accomp. 25 Cts. nett.

Louisville W. C. PETERS & C°. – PETERS, FIELD & C°. Cincinnati.

BEN BOLT,
or
AH! DON'T YOU REMEMBER.

old church yard, in the valley, Ben Bolt, In a corner obscure and a_ _lone, They have
fitted a slab of granite so gray, And sweet Alice lies un_ _der the stone. They have
ad lib.
fitted a slab of granite so gray, And sweet Alice lies un_ _der the stone.
ad lib.

3rd. V. Oh! don't you remember the school, Ben Bolt, And the Mas_ _ _ter so kind and so
2nd. V. Oh! don't you remember the wood, Ben Bolt, Near the green sun_ _ny slope of the
true, And the lit_ _ _ _ _ _tle nook by the clear running brook, Where we
hill; Where oft we have sung 'neath its wide spreading shade, And kept
gath_ _ _er'd the flow'rs as they grew. On the Mas_ _ _ _ _ _ _ _ _ter's grave grows the
time to the click of the mill: The mill has gone to de_ _
grass, Ben Bolt, And the running lit_tle brook is now dry; And of
_ _cay, Ben Bolt, And a qui_ _ _ _et now reigns all a_ _ _ _round, See the

all the friends who were school mates then, There re- - - mains Ben, but you and
old rus tic porch with its roses so sweet, Lies scatter'd and fallen to the
I. And of all the friends who were school mates then There re- -
ground, See, the old rus tic porch, with its roses so sweet, Lies
- - mains Ben, but you and I.
ad lib.
scatter'd and fallen to the ground.
ad lib.

To ALBERT G. PIKE, Esq., the Poet-Lawyer of Arkansas.

THE BONNIE BLUE FLAG

A SOUTHERN PATRIOTIC SONG,

Written, Arranged, and Sung at his "Personation Concerts,"

BY

HARRY MACARTHY,

THE ARKANSAS COMEDIAN,

Author of "Origin of the Stars and Bars,"
"The Volunteer,"
"Missouri."

NEW ORLEANS:
Published by A. E. BLACKMAR & BRO., 74 Camp Street.

COLUMBIA, S. C.,	PETERSBURG, VA.,	WILMINGTON, N. C.,	HUNTSVILLE, ALA.,
TOWNSEND & NORTH.	J. E. ROUTH.	T. S. WHITAKER.	LOGEMAN & HOLLENBERG.

THE BONNIE BLUE FLAG

HARRY MACARTHY.

_rah for the Bon_nie Blue Flag, that bears a Sin_gle Star!
CHORUS.
Hur_rah! Hur_rah! for Southern Rights Hur_rah! Hur_rah! for the
Bon_nie Blue Flag that bears a Sin_gle Star!

CHORUS. Hurrah! &c.

3rd V.

First, gallant South Carolina nobly made the stand;
Then came Alabama, who took her by the hand;
Next, quickly Mississippi, Georgia and Florida,
All rais'd on high the Bonnie Blue Flag that bears a Single Star.

CHORUS. Hurrah! &c.

4th V.

Ye men of valor, gather round the Banner of the Right,
Texas and fair Louisiana, join us in the fight;
Davis, our loved President, and Stephens, Stateman rare,
Now rally round the Bonnie Blue Flag that bears a Single Star.

CHORUS. Hurrah! &c.

5th V.

And here's to brave Virginia! the Old Dominion State
With the young Confederacy at length has link'd her fate;
Impell'd by her example, now other State prepare
To hoist on high the Bonnie Blue Flag that bears a Single Star.

CHORUS. Hurrah! &c.

6th V.

Then cheer, boys, raise the joyous shout,
For Arkansas and North Carolina now have both gone out;
And let another rousing cheer for Tennessee be given
The Single Star of the Bonnie Blue Flag has grown to be Eleven.

CHORUS. Hurrah! &c.

7th V.

Then here's to our Confederacy, strong we are and brave,
Like patriots of old, we'll fight our heritage to save;
And rather than submit to shame, to die we would prefer,
So cheer for the Bonnie Blue Flag that bears a Single Star.

CHORUS.

Hurrah! Hurrah! for Southern Rights, hurrah!
Hurrah! for the Bonnie Blue Flag has gain'd th' Eleventh Star!

Wehrmann Eng.r N.O.

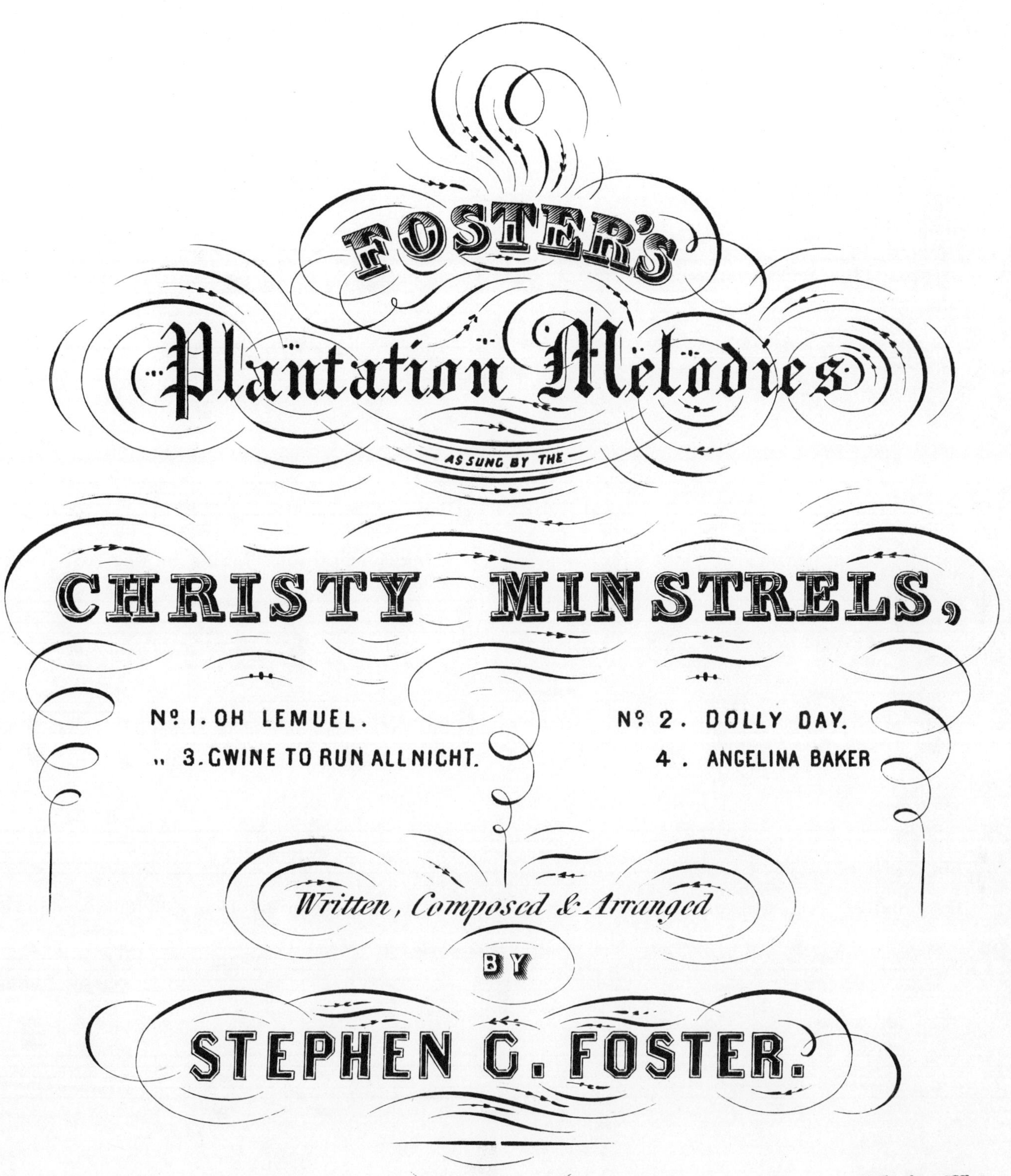

Published by F. D. BENTEEN *Baltimore.*
W. T. MAYO *New Orleans.*

"GWINE TO RUN ALL NIGHT."

or

DE CAMPTOWN RACES.

WORDS AND MUSIC BY S. C. FOSTER.

CHORUS.
go back home wid a pocket full of tin— Oh! doo-dah day!
CHORUS.
Air.
Alto.
Tenor.
Bass.
Gwine to run all night! Gwine to run all day! I'll
Gwine to run all night! Gwine to run all day! I'll
bet my money on de bob-tail nag— Somebo-dy bet on de bay.
bet my money on de bob-tail nag— Somebo-dy bet on de bay.

2

De long tail filly and de big black hoss— Doo-dah! doo-dah!
Dey fly de track and dey both cut across— Oh! doo-dah-day!
De blind hoss sticken in a big mud hole— Doo-dah! doo-dah!
Can't touch bottom wid a ten foot pole— Oh! doo-dah-day!
CHO: Gwine to run all night! &c.

3

Old muley cow come on to de track— Doo-dah! doo-dah!
De bob-tail fling her ober his back— Oh! doo-dah-day!
Den fly along like a rail-road car— Doo-dah! doo-dah!
Runnin' a race wid a shootin' star— Oh! doo-dah-day!
CHO: Gwine to run all night! &c.

4

See dem flyin' on a ten mile heat— Doo-dah! doo-dah!
Round de race track, den repeat— Oh! doo-dah-day!
I win my money on de bob-tail nag— Doo-dah! doo-dah!
I keep my money in an old tow-bag— Oh! doo-dah-day!
CHO: Gwine to run all nigh! &c.

Webb.

TWO PLANTATION MELODIES! STANDARD AND POPULAR!

CARRY ME BACK TO OLD VIRGINNY.

SONG AND CHORUS. WORDS AND MUSIC BY JAMES A. BLAND. 40.

THERE'S A HAPPY LITTLE HOME.

SONG AND CHORUS. WORDS AND MUSIC BY HARRY WOODSON. 40.

BOSTON:

OLIVER DITSON COMPANY.

NEW YORK: CHAS. H. DITSON & CO., CHICAGO: LYON & HEALY, PHILADELPHIA: J. E. DITSON & CO. BOSTON: JOHN C. HAYNES & CO.

CARRY ME BACK TO OLD VIRGINNY.

SONG AND CHORUS.

Words and Music by

JAMES BLAND.

Author of "The Old Homestead," "In the morning by the bright light," &c., &c.

There's where the old dar-ke'ys heart am long'd to go, There's where I labored so
There's where this old dar-ke'ys life will pass a-way. Mas-sa and mis-sis have
hard for old mas-sa, Day af-ter day in the field of yel-low corn,
long gone before me, Soon we will meet on that bright and gold-en shore,
ritard.
No place on earth do I love more sin-cere-ly Than old Vir-gin-ny, the state where I was born.
There we'll be hap-py and free from all sorrow, There's where we'll meet and we'll nev-er part no more.
ritard.

CHORUS.
Soprano.
Car -ry me back to old Vir-gin- ny, There's where the cotton and the corn and tatoes grow,
Alto.
Tenor.
Car -ry me back to old Vir-gin- ny, There's where the cotton and the corn and tatoes grow,
Bass.
Piano.
f
ritard. Repeat pp last time.
There's where the birds warble sweet in the spring-time, There's where this old darkey's heart am long'd to go.
ritard.
There's where the birds warble sweet in the spring-time, There's where this old darkey's heart am long'd to go.
ritard.

COMIC SONG SCHOTTISCH,

FOR CHAMPAGNE CHARLIE IS MY NAME, CHAMPAGNE CHARLIE IS MY NAME
GOOD FOR ANY GAME AT NIGHT, MY BOYS, GOOD FOR ANY GAME AT NIGHT MY BOYS.

CHAMPAGNE CHARLIE IS MY NAME, CHAMPAGNE CHARLIE IS MY NAME
GOOD FOR ANY GAME AT NIGHT, MY BOYS, WHO'LL COME AND JOIN ME IN A SPREE.

MUSIC BY

ALFRED LEE.

T. SINCLAIR'S LITH. PHIL. EACH 5

W. H. BONER & CO. 1102 Chestnut St. Philadelphia LEE & WALKER, 722 Chestnut St. CHAS W. HARRIS Troy, New York.

CHAMPAGNE CHARLIE.

Written by GEORGE LEYBOURNE. Music by ALFRED LEE.

thing I most ex - cel in is the P. R. F. G. game, A
ev - er drinks at my ex-pense are treat-ed all the same; From
Chorus.
noise all night in bed all day, and swim-ming in Cham-pagne. For
Dukes and Lords to Cab-men down, I make them drink Cham-pagne. For
ff
Champagne Charlie is my name, Champagne Charlie is my name
p
3
p
3
Good for an - y game at night my boys, good for an-y game at night my boys,
cres.
p
ff

Champagne Charlie is my name Champagne Charlie is my name
Good for an - y game at night, boys, who'll come and join me in a spree.
From Cof-fee and from sup - per rooms, from Pop-lar to Pall Mall, The
Some ep - i -cures like Bur - gun - dy, Hock, Cla -ret, and Mo - selle, But
girls on see - ing me ex - claim "Oh! what a Champagne swell!" The
Mo - et's Vin - tage on - ly sa - tis - fies this Champagne swell; What
p
ff
p
p
cres.
ff

no - tion 'tis of ev'- ry one, if 'twere not for my name, And
mat - ter if to bed I go, and head is mud - dled thick, A
Chorus.
caus-ing so much to be drunk, they'd nev - er make Cham - pagne. For
bot-tle in the morn-ing sets me right then ver - y quick. For
Champagne Charlie is my name. Champagne Charlie is my name.
Good for an - y game at night, my boys, good for an - y game at night, my boys,
ff
p
cres.

5.

Perhaps you fancy what I say is nothing else but chaff,
And only done, like other songs, to merely raise a laugh;
To prove that I am not in jest each man a bottle of Cham-
I'll stand fizz round - yes that I will, and stand it - like a lamb.
Champagne Charlie &c.

To MISS. A. C. WALKER.

SONG and CHORUS

B. R. HANBY.

BOSTON

Published by OLIVER DITSON & Co. Washington St

C. C. CLAPP & Co. Boston | J. E. GOULD. Philada | D. A. TRUAX. Cincinnati | H. D. HEWITT. N. Orleans | S. T. GORDON. N. York

PIANO. ——— GUITAR.

DARLING NELLY GRAY.

B. R. HANBY.

CHORUS.
Oh! my poor Nelly Gray, they have taken you away And I'll never see my darling any more, I'm
Oh! my poor Nelly Gray, they have taken you away And I'll never see my darling any more, I'm
sitting by the river and I'm weeping all the day, For you've gone from the old Kentucky shore.
sitting by the river and I'm weeping all the day, For you've gone from the old Kentucky shore.

3.

One night I went to see her but "she's gone!" the neighbors say,
The white man bound her with his chain,
They have taken her to Georgia for to wear her life away,
As she toils in the cotton and the cane.
Chorus.

4.

My canoe is under water and my banjo is unstrung,
I'm tired of living any more,
My eyes shall look downward and my songs shall be unsung
While I stay on the old Kentucky shore.
Chorus.

5.

My eyes are getting blinded and I cannot see my way,
Hark! there's somebody knocking at the door —
Oh! I hear the angels calling and I see my Nelly Gray,
Farewell to the old Kentucky shore.

Chorus, to the last verse.

Oh! my darling Nelly Gray, up in heaven there they say,
That they'll never take you from me any more,
I'm a coming — coming — coming, as the angels clear the way,
Farewell to the old Kentucky shore.

To E. F. Dixey Esq.

DER

DEITCHER'S DOG

Comic Ballad

BY

SEP. WINNER.

Geo. F. Swain.

Philadelphia

Published by SEP. WINNER 933 Sp. Garden St.

DER DEITCHER'S DOG

CHORUS.

AIR.
Tra la la la la la la la la la la, la la la la la la la la la
ALTO.
Tra la la la la la la la la, la la la la la la
TENOR.
Tra la la la la la la la la, la la la la la la
BASS.
Tra la la la, la la la
PIANO.
la, Tra la la la la la la la la la la Tra la la la la la la. . . .
la. la la la la la la la la la la la la la. . . .
la, la la la la la la la la la la la la la. . . .
la, la la la la Tra la la. . . .

2 I loves mine la_ _ger 'tish ve_ry goot beer, Oh where, Oh where can he be . . . . But mit no mon_ey I can_not drink here. Oh where, Oh where ish he . . . .
3 A_cross the o_cean in Gar_ _ma_nie, Oh where, Oh where can he be . . . . Der deitch_ _ers dog ish der best com_pan_ie. Oh where, Oh where ish he . . . .
4 Un sas_age ish goot, bo_lo_nie of course, Oh where, Oh where can he be . . . . Dey makes um mit dog und dey makes em mit horse, I guess de makes em mit he . . . .

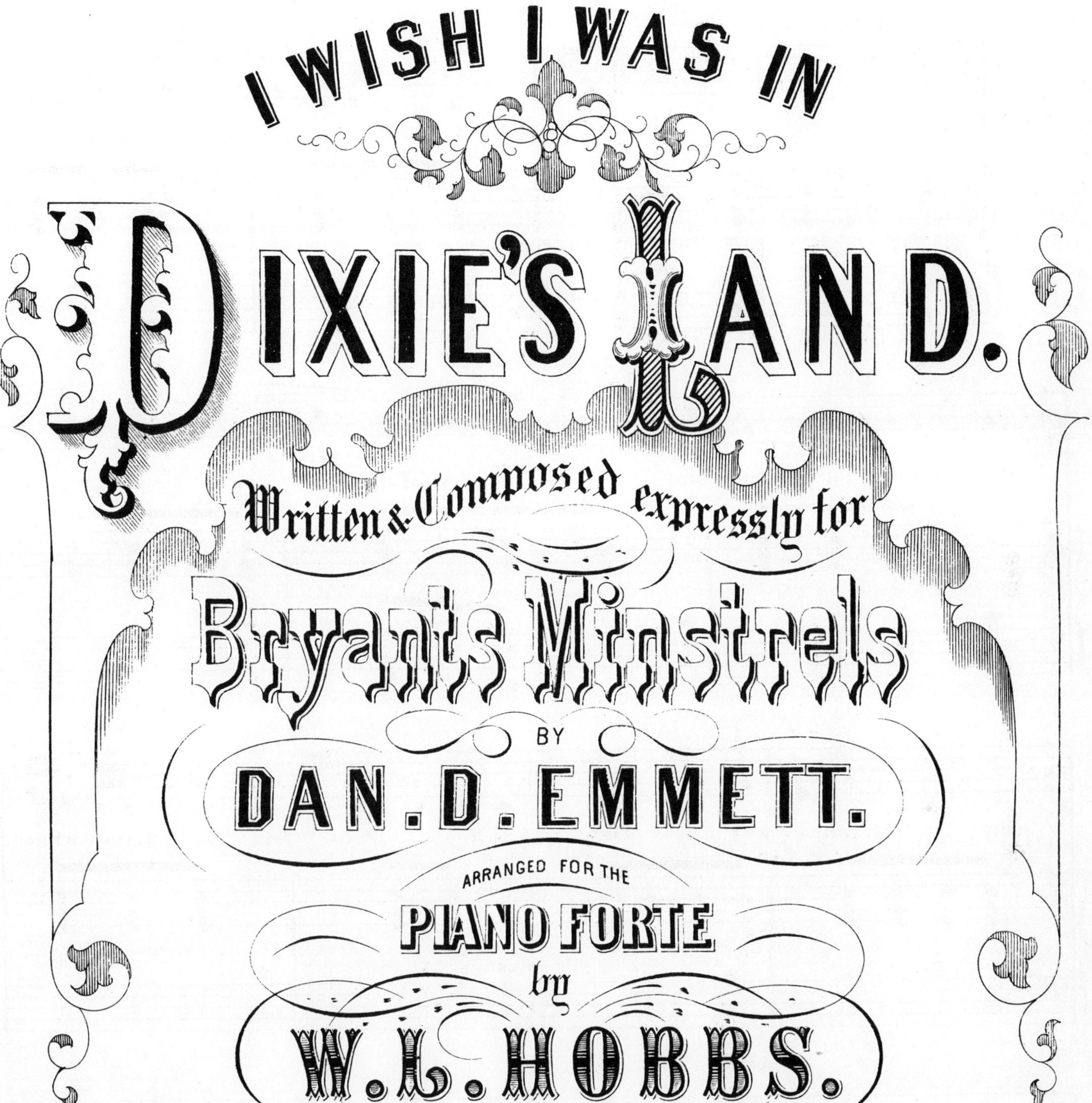

2½

NEW YORK
Published by FIRTH, POND & CO. *547 Broadway.*

Boston, O. DITSON & CO. | *Cincinnati,* C. Y. FONDA. | *Pittsburgh,* H. KLEBER & BRO.

DIXIE'S LAND

COMPOSED BY DAN' EMMETT. ARRANGED BY W. L. HOBBS.

way! Look a - way! Look a - way! Dix - ie Land.
CHORUS.
Den I wish I was in Dix - ie, Hoo - ray! Hoo - ray! In Dix - ie Land, I'll
took my stand, To lib an die in Dix - ie, A - way, A - way, A -
way down south in Dix - ie, A - way, A - way, A - way down south in Dix - ie.

2.

Old Missus marry "Will-de-weaber,"
Willium was a gay deceaber;
Look away! &c_
But when he put his arm around'er,
He smilled as fierce as a 'forty-pound'er.
Look away! &c_
*Chorus*_ Den I wish I was in Dixie, &c_

3.

His face was sharp as a butchers cleaber,
But dat did not seem to greab'er;
Look away! &c_
Old Missus acted de foolish part,
And died for a man dat broke her heart.
Look away! &c_
*Chorus*_ Den I wish I was in Dixie, &c_

4.

Now here's a health to the next old Missus,
An all de galls dat want to kiss us;
Look away! &c_
But if you want to drive 'way sorrow,
Come an hear dis song to-morrow.
Look away! &c_
*Chorus*_ Den I wish I was in Dixie, &c_

5.

Dar's buck-wheat cakes an 'Ingen' batter,
Makes you fat or a little fatter;
Look away! &c_
Den hoe it down an scratch your grabble,
To Dixie land I'm bound to trabble.
Look away! &c_
*Chorus*_ Den I wish I was in Dixie, &c_

DOWN IN ALABAM

OR

(AINT I GLAD I GOT OUT DE WILDERNESS.)

ETHIOPIAN REFRAIN

AS SUNG BY

Bryant's Minstrels

Melody by

J. WARNER.

HARMONIZED & ARRANGED BY

WALTER MEADOWS.

2½

NEW YORK

Published by WM. HALL & SON *543 Broadway.*

Boston HENRY TOLMAN. *Marysville, Cal.* G. AMY. D.P. FAULDS & CO. *Louisville.*

DOWN IN ALABAM'

or

"AINT I GLAD I GOT OUT DE WILDERNESS."

Words and Music by J. WARNER.

Arranged by WALTER MEADOWS.

Lively.

All the voices.

Ah! Ah! Ah! Ah!

sf *sf*

SOLO.
My old mas - sa he's got the dropser, um, he's got the dropser, um, he's got the dropser, um,
He am sure to die 'kase he's got no doc-tor, um, Down in Al - a - bam'.
CHORUS.
1st Voice.
Aint I glad I got out de wil - der-ness, Got out de wil-der-ness,
2nd Voice.
Aint I glad I got out de wil - der- ness, Got out de wil-der-ness,
3rd Voice.
Aint I glad I got out de wil - der-ness, Got out de wil-der-ness,
PIANO.

Go back to Symphony.

2

Old blind horse come from Jerusalum,
Come from Jerusalum,
Come from Jerusalum
He kicks so high dey put him in de museum,
Down in Alabam'.
Chorus:

3

Dis am a holiday, we hab assembled, um,
We hab assembled, um,
We hab assembled, um
To dance and sing for de ladies and genbleum,
Down in Alabam'.
Chorus:

4

Far you well to de wild goose nation,
Wild goose nation,
Wild goose nation,
I neber will leab de old plantation,
Down in Alabam'.
Chorus:

NEW-YORK.
C.H. DITSON & CO _ 711 Broadway.

Chicago. Lyon & Healy. Boston. Ditson & Co. Boston, J.C. Haynes & Co.
Cinn. J. Church Jr. Phil^a. C.W.A. Trumpler.

THE FLYING TRAPEZE.

* Chorus for last verse.

3

Her father and mother were both on my side,
And very hard tried to make her my own bride;
Her father he sighed, and her mother she cried,
To see her throw herself away.
'Twas all no avail, she went there every night,
And would throw him boquets on the stage,
Which caus'd him to meet her; how he ran me down,
To tell you, would take a whole page.

4

One night I as usual, went to her dear home,
Found there her father and mother alone;
I ask'd for my love, and soon they made known,
To my horror, that she'd run away!
She'd pack'd up her box, and eloped in the night
With him, with the greatest of ease;
From two storys high, he had lowered her down
To the ground on his flying Trapeze!

5

Some months after this I went to a Hall;
Was greatly surprised to see on the wall
A bill in red letters, which did my heart gall,
That she was appearing with him:
He taught her gymnastics, and dressed her in tights,
To help him to live at his ease,
And made her assume a masculine name,
And now she goes on the Trapeze!

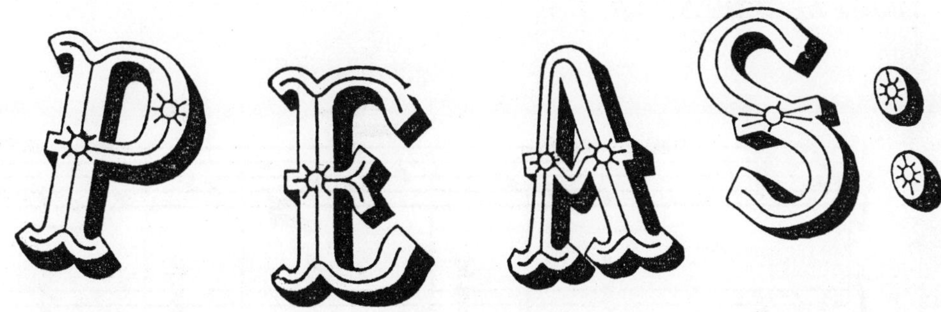

WORDS BY A. PINDAR, ESQ.

MUSIC BY P. NUTT, ESQ.

NEW ORLEANS:

Published by A. E. BLACKMAR, 167 Canal Street.

GOOBER PEAS.

Words by A. PINDAR, Esq. *Music by P. NUTT, Esq.*

mf

1. Sit - ting by the road-side on a sum-mer day, Chat - ting with my mess-mates
2. When a horse-man pass - es, the soldiers have a rule, To cry out at their loud - est

pass - ing time a - way, Ly - ing in the shadow un - der- neath the trees,
"Mis - ter here's your mule," But an - oth - er pleasure en - chant-ing - er than these, Is

3.

Just before the battle the General hears a row,
He says "the Yanks are coming, I hear their rifles now,
He turns around in wonder, and what do you think he sees
The Georgia Militia, eating goober peas!

Chorus.

4.

I think my song has lasted almost long enough,
The subject's interesting, but rhymes are mighty rough,
I wish this war was over when free from rags and fleas,
We'd kiss our wives and sweethearts and gobble goober peas!

Chorus.

GRAND-FATHER'S CLOCK.

Song and Chorus.

WORDS AND MUSIC BY

HENRY C. WORK.

GUITAR. 

PIANO.

NEW YORK:

Published by C. M. CADY, 107 Duane St.

To my Sister Lizzie.

GRANDFATHER'S CLOCK.

Words and Music by HENRY C. WORK.

No. 52.

wast - ed no time, and had but one de-sire— At the close of each week to be wound. And it
knew that his spir - it was plum - ing for flight—That his hour of de - parture had come. Still the
tall - er by half than the old man himself, Though it weighed not a pennyweight more. It was
childhood and man - hood the clock seemed to know And to share both his grief and his joy. For it
kept in its place—not a frown up - on its face, And its hands nev - er hung by its side; But it
clock kept the time, with a soft and muffled chime, As we si - lent - ly stood by his side; But it
bought on the morn of the day that he was born, And was al - ways his treasure and pride; But it
struck twenty-four when he en-tered at the door, With a bloom-ing and beau - ti - ful bride; But it
stopp'd short— nev - er to go a - gain— When the old man died.
stopp'd short— nev - er to go a - gain— When the old man died.
stopp'd short— nev - er to go a - gain— When the old man died.
stopp'd short— nev - er to go a - gain— When the old man died.

CHORUS.

In exact time.
Nine-ty years, with-out slumber-ing (tick, tick, tick, tick), His life - seconds num-ber-ing (tick, tick, tick, tick), It
Nine-ty years, with-out slumber-ing (tick, tick, tick, tick), His life - seconds num-ber-ing (tick, tick, tick, tick), It
stopp'd short— nev - er to go a - gain— When the old man died.
stopp'd short— nev - er to go a - gain— When the old man died.

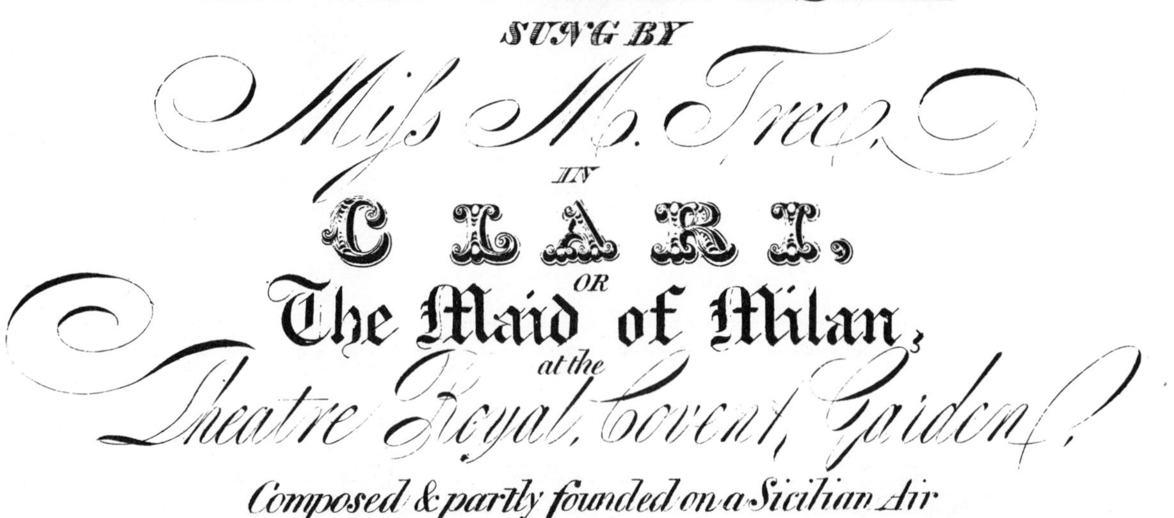

HOME! SWEET HOME!

SUNG BY

Miss M. Tree,

IN

CLARI,

OR

The Maid of Milan,

at the

Theatre Royal, Covent, Garden.

Composed & partly founded on a Sicilian Air

BY

HENRY R. BISHOP.

Pr: 25.

Philadelphia, Published by G.E.Blake No 13 south Fifth Street.

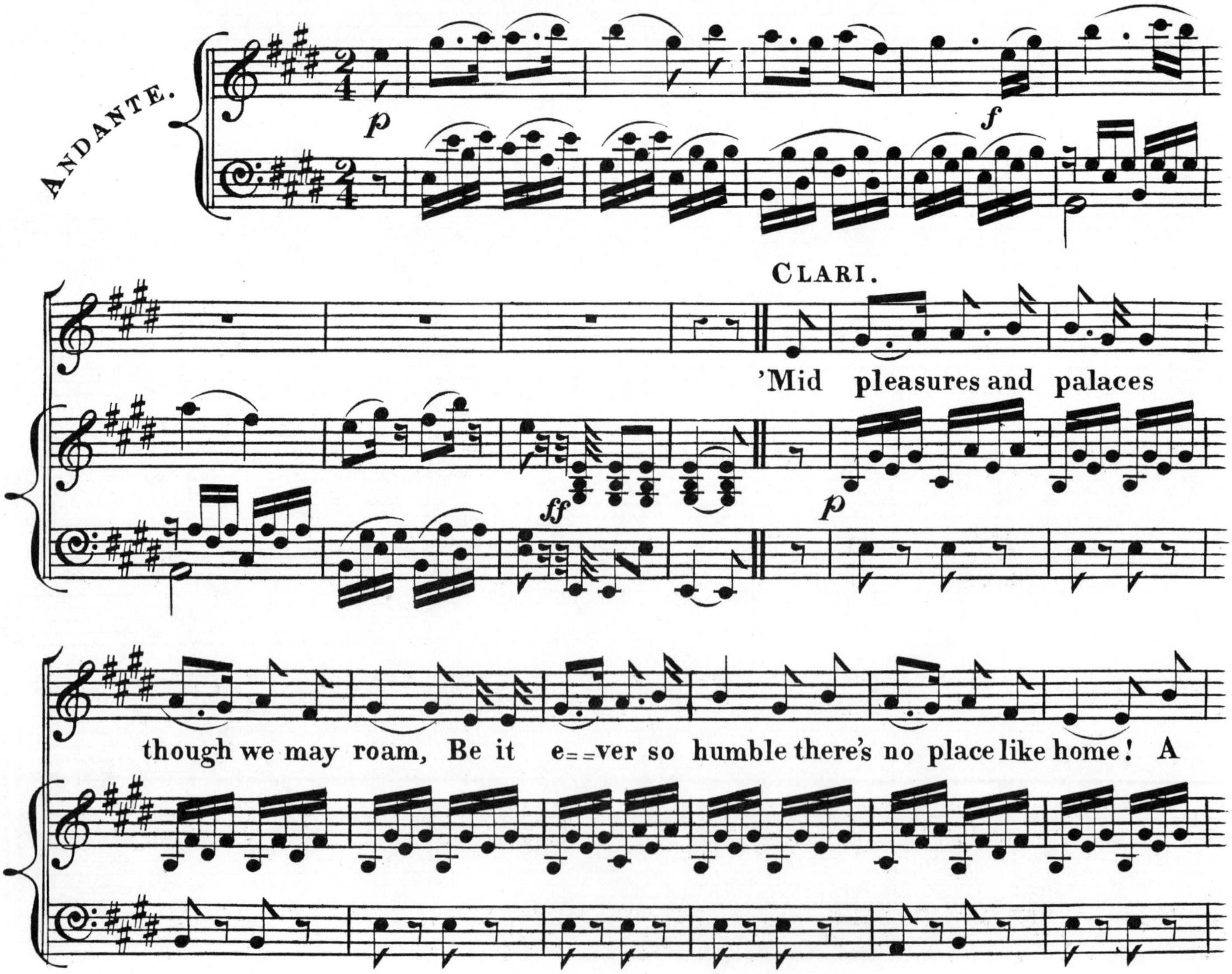
ANDANTE.
p
f
CLARI.
ff
p
'Mid pleasures and palaces
though we may roam, Be it e=-ver so humble there's no place like home! A

charm from the skies seems to hal_low us there, Which seek through the
world, is ne'er met with else = where: Home! Home! sweet, sweet,
Espress
pp
Home! There's no place like Home! There's no place like Home!
Largo
pp
colla voce
ff ten
Tempo 1o
2d VERSE. piu animato.
An ex = ile from Home, splendour dazzles in
ff
p

Espress:
vain, Oh! give me my low=ly thatch'd cottage a===gain! The
birds singing gaily that came at my call, Give me them with the
peace of mind, dearer than all: Home! Home! sweet, sweet
Home! There's no place like Home! There's no place like Home!
Largo
ad lib:
colla voce
pp
ff
ten:

I'LL TAKE YOU HOME AGAIN, KATHLEEN.

SONG AND CHORUS.

WORDS AND MUSIC BY

THOMAS P. WESTENDORF.

4

CINCINNATI.

Published by JOHN CHURCH & CO. 66 W. Fourth St.

CHICAGO. ROOT & SONS MUSIC CO.

NEW YORK. J. CHURCH & CO.

I'll Take You Home Again, Kathleen.

Words and Music by THOMAS P. WESTENDORF.

first you were my bon - ny bride. The ro - - ses all have left your
life holds noth - ing dear but you. The smiles that once you gave to
lov - - ing heart will cease to yearn. Where laughs the lit - tle sil - ver
f
cheek, I've watched them fade a - way and die; Your
me, I scarce - - ly ev - er see them now, Tho'
stream, Be - side your moth - er's hum - ble cot, And
p
voice is sad when e'er you speak, And tears be - dim your lov - ing eyes.
ma - - ny, ma - ny times I see A dark - - 'ning sha - dow on your brow.
bright - est rays of sun - shine gleam, There all your grief will be for - got.

CHORUS.
Sop.
Oh! I will take you back, Kath-leen, To where your heart will feel no pain, And
Alto.
Oh! Take you back, Kath-leen, Heart will feel no pain,
Tenor.
Oh! Take you back, Kath-leen, Heart will feel no pain
Bass.
Piano.
when the fields are fresh and green, I'll take you to your home a - gain.
Fields are fresh and green, Take you to your home a-gain, home a-gain.
Fields are fresh and green, Take you to your home a-gain, home a-gain.

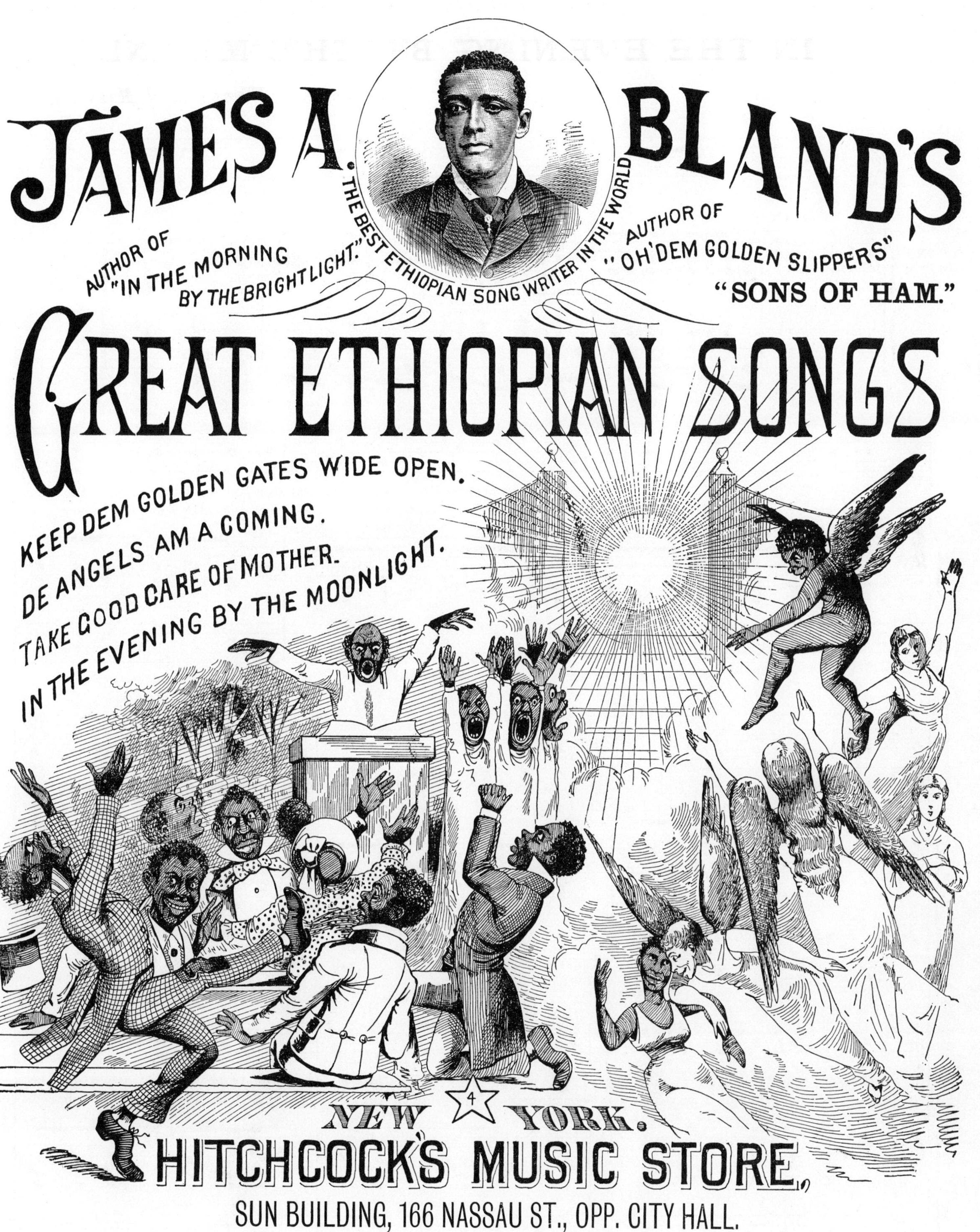

Hitchcock's New Music Store, 283 Sixth Ave., near 18th St.

Dedicated to Mr. NEIL MOORE,

IN THE EVENING BY THE MOONLIGHT.

Words and Music by JAS. BLAND.

hung up - on de wall, While de sil - v'ry moon was shin - ing clear and bright, How de
ne'er re - turn a - gain, Eb - 'ry thing was den so mer - ry gay and bright, And I
old folks would en - joy it, they would sit all night and lis - ten, As we sang in de ebe-'ning by de moon - light.
neb - er will for - get it, when our dai - ly toil was o - ber, How we sang in de ebe-'ning by de moon - light.
CHORUS.
SOPRANO.
In de ebe - ning by de moon - light, you could hear us dar - kies sing - ing, In de
ALTO.
TENOR.
In de ebe - ning by de moon - light, you could hear us dar - kies sing - ing, In de
BASS.
Piano

ebe-ning by de moon-light you could hear de ban - jo ringing, How de old folks would en - joy it, They would
ebe-ning by de moon-light you could hear de ban - jo ringing, How de old folks would en - joy it, They would
sit all night and lis - ten, As we sang in de ebe-ning by de moon - light.
sit all night and lis - ten, As we sang in de ebe-ning by de moon - light.

THE VIRGINIA MINSTRELS,

No. 3

"JIM CRACK CORN"

or the Blue tail Fly,

composed for the

PIANO FORTE.

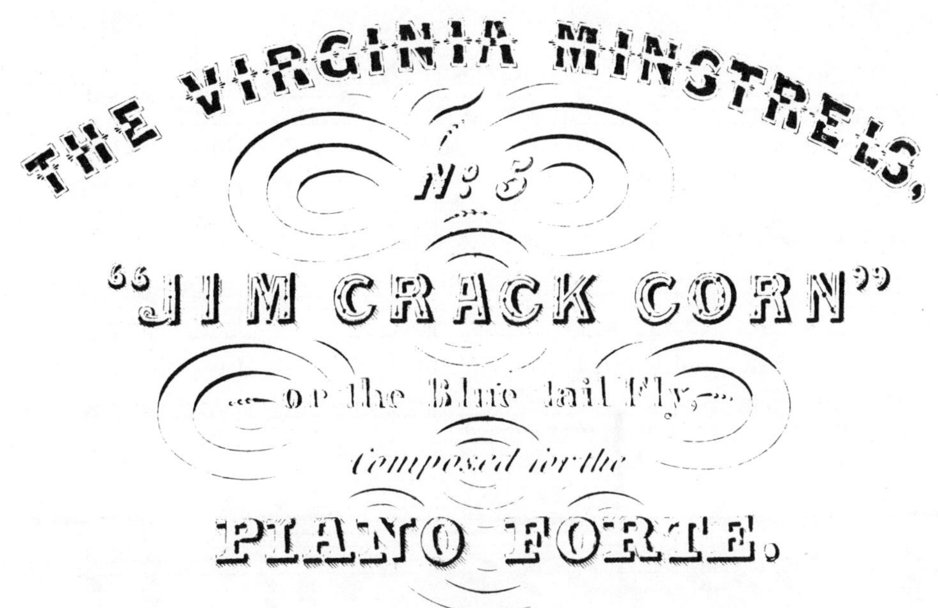

Published by F. D. BENTEEN *Baltimore.*

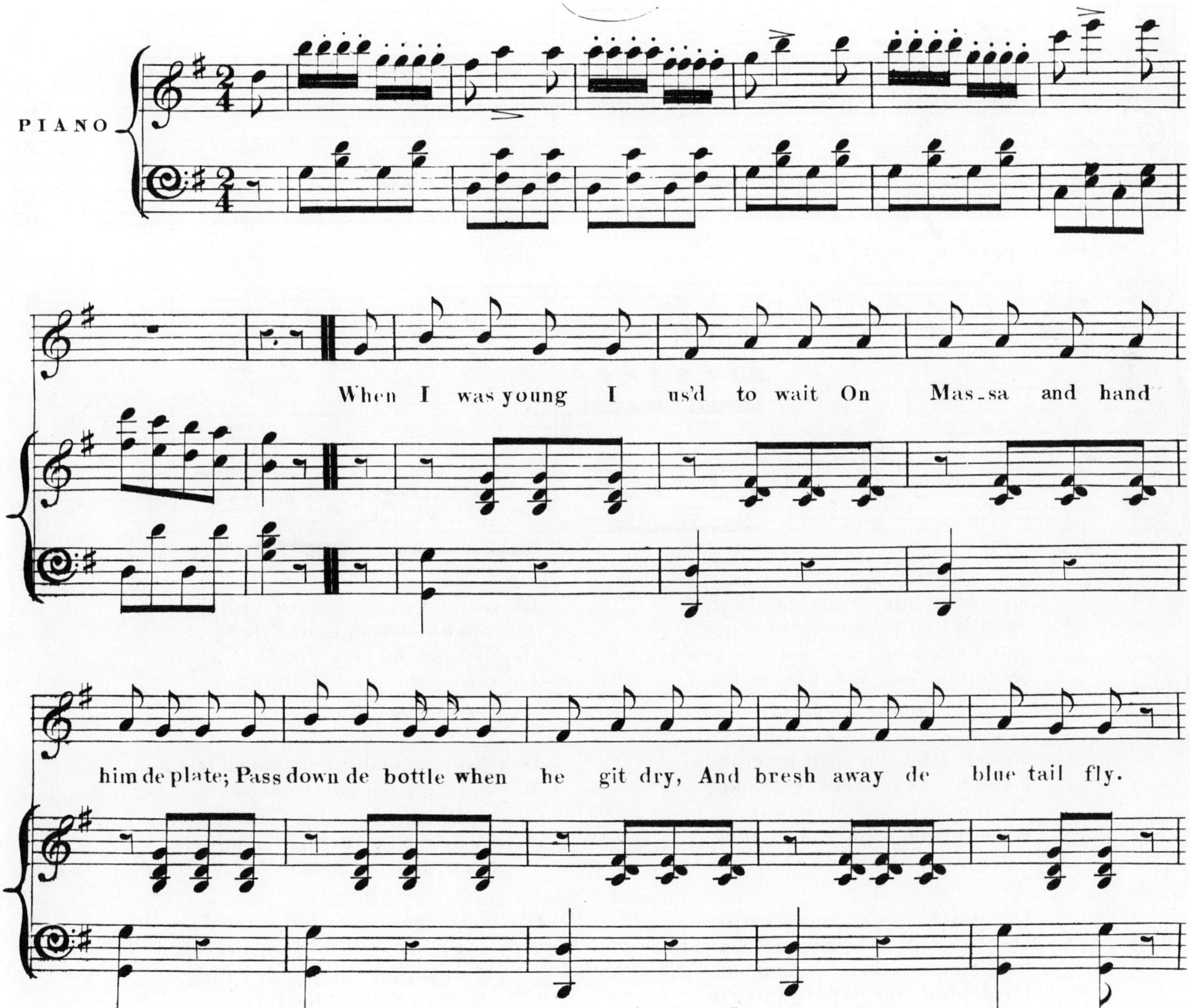
PIANO
When I was young I us'd to wait On Mas-sa and hand
him de plate; Pass down de bottle when he git dry, And bresh away de blue tail fly.

2.
Den arter dinner massa sleep,
He bid dis niggar vigil keep;
An' when he gwine to shut his eye,
He tell me watch de blue tail fly.
Jim crack corn &c.

3.
An' when he ride in de arternoon,
I foller wid a hickory broom;
De poney being berry shy,
When bitten by de blue tail fly.
Jim crack corn &c.

4.
One day he rode aroun' de farm,
De flies so numerous dey did swarm;
One chance to bite 'im on the thigh,
De debble take dat blu tail fly.
Jim crack corn &c.

5.
De poney run, he jump an' pitch,
An' tumble massa in de ditch;
He died, an' de jury wonder'd why
De verdic was de blue tail fly.
Jim crack corn &c.

6.
Dey laid 'im under a 'simmon tree,
His epitaph am dar to see:
'Beneath dis stone I'm forced to lie,
All by de means ob de blue tail fly.
Jim crack corn &c.

7.
Ole massa gone, now let 'im rest,
Dey say all tings am for de best;
I nebber forget till de day I die,
Ole massa an' dat blue tail fly.
Jim crack corn &c.

Webb.

J. C. Haynes & Co. Boston. | Cinn. | C. W. A. Trumpler. Phil.ª
W. A. Pond & Co. N. York | J. Church Jr. | Lyon & Healy. Chicago

THE ONE HORSE OPEN SLEIGH.

J. PIERPONT.

CHORUS.
SOP:
ALTO
TENOR
BASS
Piano
Jingle bells, Jingle bells, Jingle all the way; Oh! what joy it
Jingle bells, Jingle bells, Jingle all the way; Oh! what joy it
is to ride In a one horse o - pen sleigh. Jingle bells, Jingle bells,
is to ride In a one horse o - pen sleigh. Jingle bells, Jingle bells,
8va

3.

A day or two ago,
The story I must tell
I went out on the snow
And on my back I fell;
A gent was riding by
In a one horse open sleigh,
He laughed as there I sprawling lie,
But quickly drove away.

4.

Now the ground is white
Go it while you're young,
Take the girls to night
And sing this sleighing song;
Just get a bob tailed bay
Two forty as his speed.
Hitch him to an open sleigh
And crack, you'll take the lead.

JOHNNY GET YOUR GUN.

Ethiopian Song and Chorus.

ORIGINATED AND SUNG BY

AMERICA'S POPULAR COMEDIANS,

SHEFFER AND BLAKELY,

AND WRITTEN FOR THEM BY 4

 **F. BELASCO,** 

SONG (M. H. ROSENFELD.) POLKA.

NEW YORK:
Published by T. B. HARMS & CO., 819 Broadway.
ST. LOUIS, MO.:
CHARLES I. WYNNE & CO.

"JOHNNY GET YOUR GUN."

Song and Chorus.

By F. BELASCO.
(M. H. ROSENFELD.)

gun, I met old Pe - ter on de way, Johnny get your gun, get your
gun, And but - ton on your gold - en vest, Johnny get your gun, get your
gun, We'll shoot old Sa - tan 'fore he scoots, Johnny get your gun, get your
gun, Said he, "I'll want you by an' by, Johnny get your gun, get your
gun, ... Mo - ses wept and A - bram cried, Johnny get your gun, get your
gun, ... Tell your Un - cles and your Aunts, Johnny get your gun, get your
gun, ... When you hear de ras - cal yell, Johnny get your gun, get your
gun, ... Fetch me up an Al - der - man, Johnny get your gun, get your
gun, Sa - tan's com-ing don't you hide, Johnny get your gun, get your gun.......
gun, Fetch a - long their lin - en pants, Johnny get your gun, get your gun.......
gun, Aim your mus ket, give him- well, Jonnny get your gun, get your gun.......
gun, Put him in my fry - ing pan, Johnny get your gun, get your gun.......

Refrain.
Johnny get your gun, get your gun to-day, Pig-eons a fly-ing
all the way, If you want to get to Heav-en in de good ole way,
John-ny get your gun, get your gun!
Chorus.
f
Roll-ing on, Roll-ing on to glo-ry chil-dren

Roll ing on, John - ny get your gun, get your gun!............
Dance.
Vivace.
mf
f
Wm. H. Keyser & Co., Music Typographers, 921 Arch St., Phila.

Song & Chorus

by

GEO. F. ROOT.

Published by ROOT & CADY 95 Clark St.

CHICAGO.

JUST BEFORE THE BATTLE, MOTHER.

Words & Music by GEO. F. ROOT.

✲ In the Army of the Cumberland, the Soldiers sing the Battle-Cry when going into action, by order of the Commanding General.

CHORUS
Fare-well Mother, you may nev-er Press me to your heart a-gain; But
Fare-well Mother, you may nev-er you may nev-er Mother Press me to your heart a-gain;... But
Fare-well Mother, you may nev-er you may nev-er Mother Press me to your heart a-gain;... But
repeat pp.
O, you'll not for-get me, Mother, If I'm number'd with the slain.
ritard.
O, you'll not for-get me, Mother, you will not for-get me, If I'm number'd with the slain.
O, you'll not for-get me, Mother, you will not for-get me, If I'm number'd with the slain.
ritard.

Twentieth Edition.

SONG AND CHORUS,

—BY—

HENRY C. WORK.

AUTHOR OF

"Nellie Lost and Found;" "Our Captain's Last Words;" "Grafted into the Army, etc."

CHICAGO:

Published by ROOT & CADY, 95 Clark Street.

WM. HALL & SON, FIRTH, POND & CO., New York. HENRY TOLMAN & CO., Boston. S. BRAINARD & CO., Cleveland.

H. N. HEMPSTED, Milwaukee. J. H. WHITTEMORE, Detroit.

KINGDOM COMING.

Words and Music by HENRY C. WORK.

CHORUS.

Air.
spec he's run a - way! De mas - sa run? ha, ha! De' dar - key stay? ho,
Alto.
Tenor.
De mas - sa run? ha, ha! De dar - key stay? ho,
Bass.
ho! It mus' be now de king - dom com - in', An' de year ob Ju - bi - lo!
ho! It mus' be now de king - dom com - in', An' de year ob Ju - bi - lo!

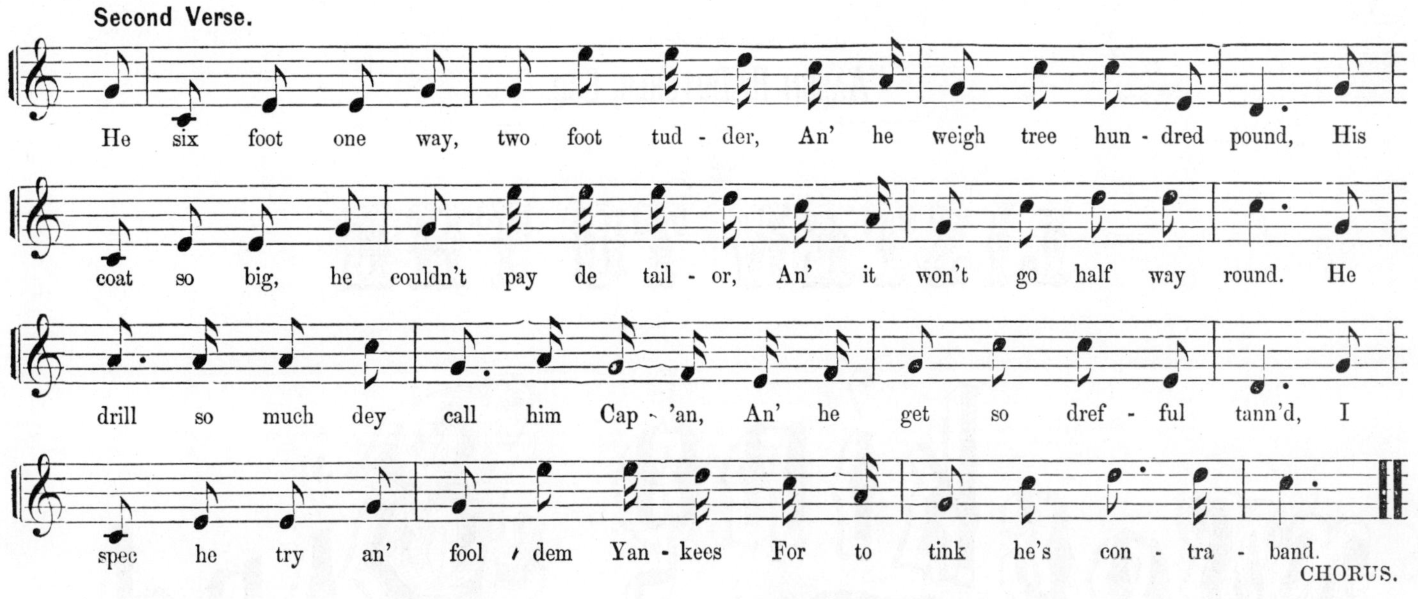
Second Verse.
He six foot one way, two foot tud - der, An' he weigh tree hun - dred pound, His
coat so big, he couldn't pay de tail - or, An' it won't go half way round. He
drill so much dey call him Cap - 'an, An' he get so dref - ful tann'd, I
spec he try an' fool dem Yan - kees For to tink he's con - tra - band.
CHORUS.

Third Verse.
De dar - keys feel so lone - some lib - ing in de log - house on de lawn, Dey
move dar tings to mas - sa's par - lor For to keep it while he's gone. Dar's
wine an' ci - der in de kit - chen, An' de dar - keys dey'll hab some; I
spose dey'll all be corn - fis - ca - ted When de Lin - kum so - jers come. CHORUS.

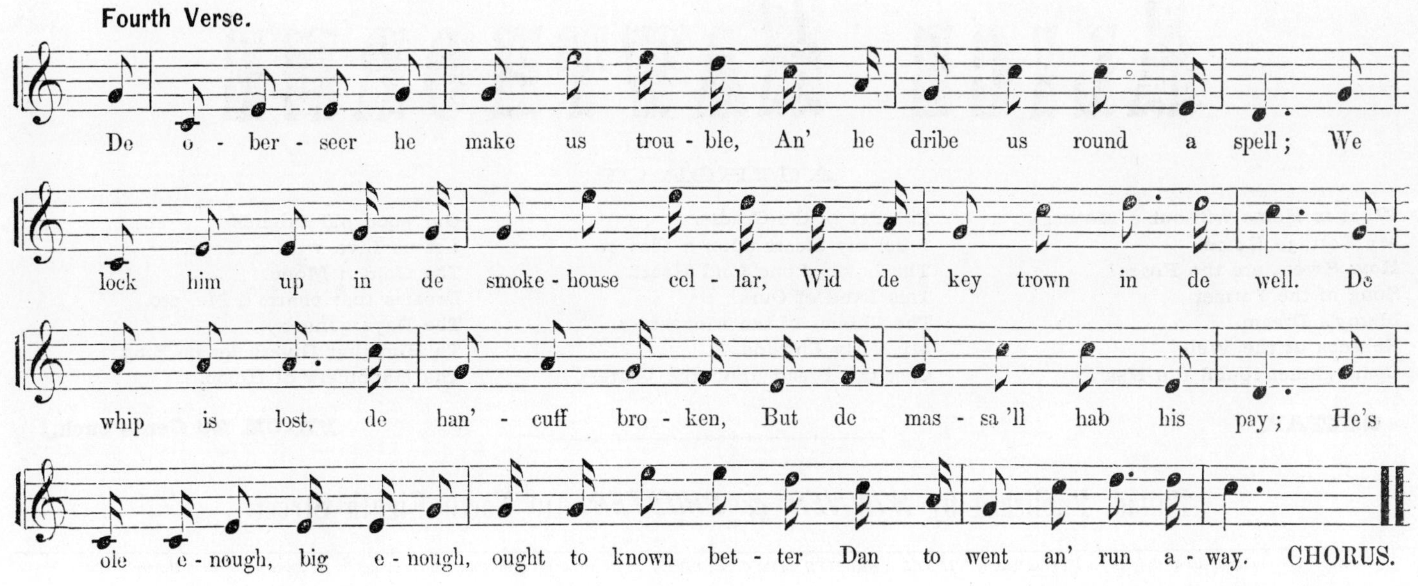
Fourth Verse.
De o - ber - seer he make us trou - ble, An' he dribe us round a spell; We
lock him up in de smoke - house cel - lar, Wid de key trown in de well. De
whip is lost, de han' - cuff bro - ken, But de mas - sa 'll hab his pay; He's
ole e - nough, big e - nough, ought to known bet - ter Dan to went an' run a - way. CHORUS.

Respectfully dedicated to

AARON R. DUTCHER, ESQ.

LISTEN TO THE

MELODY

By

RICHARD MILBURN

Written and arranged by

ALICE HAWTHORNE

AUTHOR OF

What is Home without a Mother?
My Cottage Home.
How Sweet are the Roses!
Song of the Farmer.
Mercy's Dream.
Rebecca at the Well.
Come gather round the Hearth.

The Pet of the Cradle.
I Set my Heart upon a Flower.
The Love of one fond Heart.
This Land of Ours.
The Chimes of the Monastery.
My Early Fireside.
Cast thy Bread upon the Waters.

Our good old Friends.
Let us Live with a Hope.
The Golden Moon.
Dreams that charm'd Me, etc.
The Days gone by.
To Him that Giveth let us Sing.
The Happiness of Home.

GUITAR. **PRICE, 25 Cents each.**

Philad. Published by *WINNER & SHUSTER,* 110 North Eighth Street.

LISTEN TO THE MOCKING BIRD.

BY

ALICE HAWTHORNE.

3. When the charms of spring a - wa - ken, ... a - wa - ken, ... a - wa - ken : . . . . . When the
VOICE.
1. I'm dream - ing now of Hal - ly, ... sweet Hal - ly, ... sweet Hal - ly ; . . . . I'm
2. Ah ! well I yet re - mem - ber, . . . re - mem - ber, . . . re - mem - ber, . . . Ah !
PIANO.
charms of spring a - wa - ken, ... And the mock - ing bird is sing - ing on the bough. I
dream - ing now of Hal - ly, ... For the thought of her is one that ne - ver dies : She's
well I yet re - mem - ber, ... When we ga - ther'd in the cot - ton side by side ; 'Twas
feel like one for - sak - en, ... for - sak - en, ... for - sak - en. I
sleep - ing in the val - ley, ... the val - ley, ... the val - ley ; . . . . . She's
in the mild Sep - tem - ber, ... Sep - tem - ber, ... Sep - tem - ber, ... 'Twas
feel like one for - sak - en, ... Since my Hal - ly is no long - er with me now. . . . .
sleep - ing ing the val - ley, ... And the mock - ing bird is sing - ing where she lies. . . . .
in the mild Sep - tem - ber, ... And the mock - ing bird was sing - ing far and wide. . . . .

CHORUS.
SOLO.
Listen to the mocking bird, Listen to the mocking bird, The mocking bird still sing-ing o'er her
PIANO.
grave; Listen to the mocking bird, Listen to the mocking bird, Still singing where the weeping willows wave.
QUARTETTE.
AIR.
Listen to the mock-ing bird, Listen to the mock-ing bird, The mock-ing bird still sing-ing o'er her
ALTO.
TENOR.
Listen to the mock-ing bird, Listen to the mock-ing bird, The mock-ing bird still sing-ing o'er her
BASS.
8va
PIANO.

grave; Listen to the mocking bird, Listen to the mocking bird, Still sing-ing where the weep-ing wil-lows wave.
grave; Listen to the mocking bird, Listen to the mocking bird, Still sing-ing where the weeping wil-lows wave.
8va
tr
8va
tr

THE LITTLE BROWN JUG

SONG AND CHORUS.

BY

EASTBURN

PIANO

GUITAR.

PHILADELPHIA:

Published by J. E. WINNER, 545 North Eighth St.

LEE & WALKER, 922 Chestnut Street.

THE LITTLE BROWN JUG.

EASTBURN.

CHORUS.
AIR.
Ha, ha, ha, you and me, "Lit-tle brown jug" don't I love thee;
ALTO.
TENOR.
Ha, ha, ha, you and me, "Lit-tle brown jug" don't I love thee.
BASS.
PIANO
Ha, ha, ha, you and me, "Lit-tle brown jug" don't I love thee.
Ha, ha, ha, you and me, "Lit-tle brown jug" don't I love thee.

3. When I go toiling to my farm,
I take little "Brown Jug" under my arm;
I place it under a shady tree,
Little "Brown Jug" 'tis you and me.—*Cho.*

4. If all the folks in Adam's race,
Were gathered together in one place;
Then I'd prepare to shed a tear,
Before I'd part from you, my dear.—*Cho.*

5. If I'd a cow that gave such milk,
I'd clothe her in the finest silk;
I'd feed her on the choicest hay,
And milk her forty times a day.—*Cho.*

6. The rose is red, my nose is, too,
The violet's blue, and so are you;
And yet I guess before I stop,
We'd better take another drop.—*Cho.*

J. M. Armstrong, Music Typographer, No. 121 S. Seventh St., Philada.

LONG, LONG AGO!

A Ballad

Composed by

TH. H. BAYLY, ESQ.

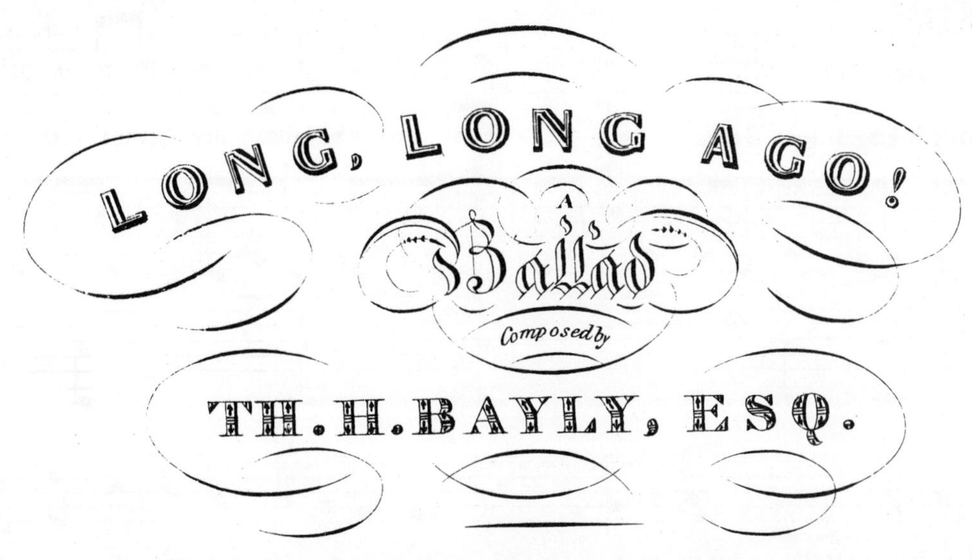

New York Firth & Hall 1 Franklin Square.

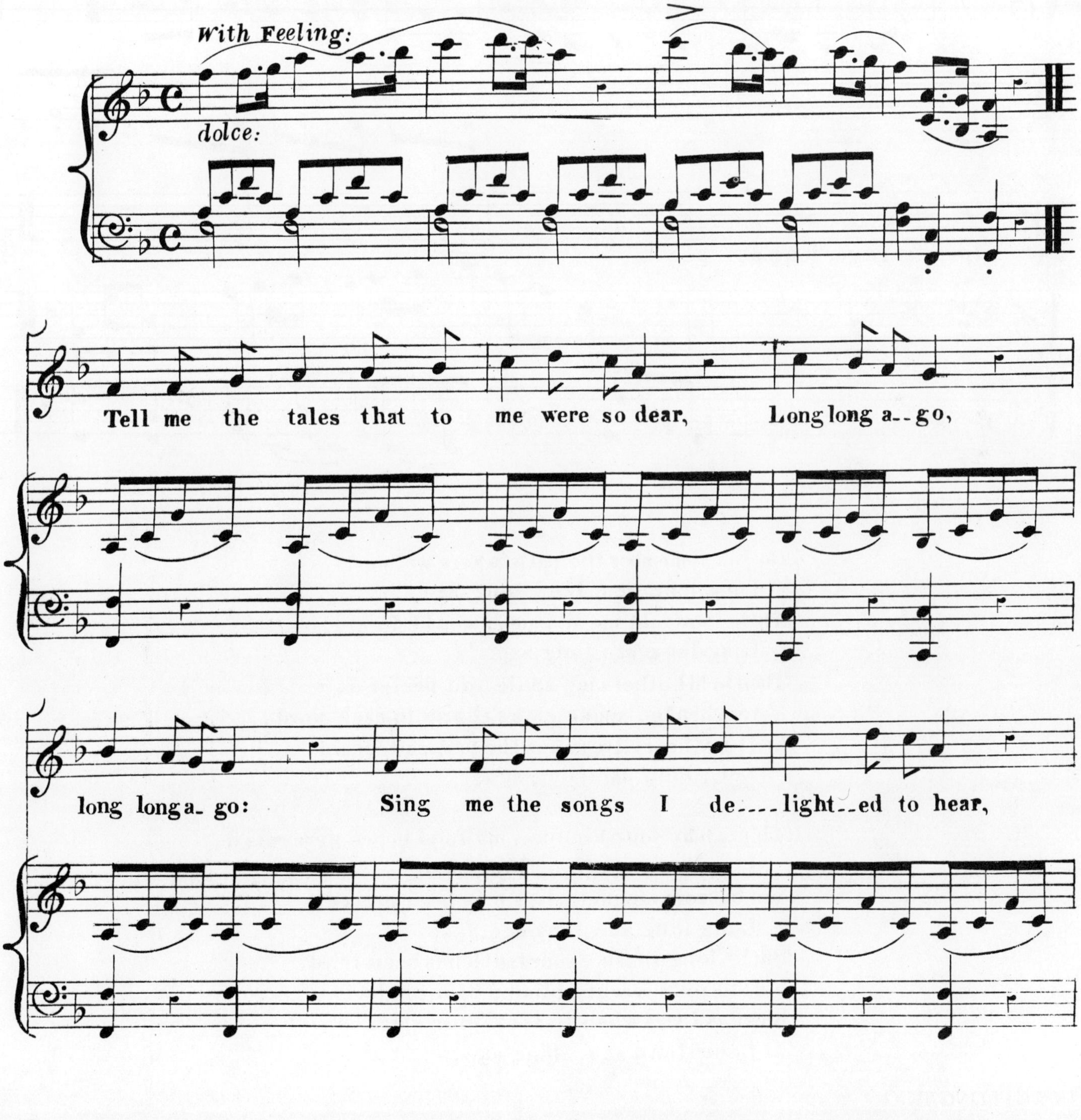
With Feeling:
dolce:
Tell me the tales that to me were so dear, Long long a--go,
long long a- go: Sing me the songs I de----light--ed to hear,

2

Do you remember the path where we met,
Long long ago, long long ago.
Ah yes you told me you ne'er would forget,
Long long ago, long ago.
Then to all others my smile you prefer'd,
Love when you spoke gave a charm to each word,
Still my heart treasures the praises I heard,
Long long ago, long ago,

3

Though by your kindness my fond hopes were rais'd,
Long long ago, long long ago,
You by more eloquent lips have been prais'd,
Long long ago, long ago,
But by long absence your truth has been tried,
Still to your accents I listen with pride,
Blest as I was when I sat by your side,
Long long ago, long ago,

Guitar.

Piano.

CHICAGO,

Published by **H.M. HIGGINS**, 117 Randolph St.

"LORENA."

Poetry by REV. H. D. L. WEBSTER.
Music by J. P. WEBSTER.
ANDANTE ESPRESSIVO.
1. The
2. A
years creep slowly by, Lo-re - - na, The snow is on the grass a-gain, The
hun-dred months have pass'd Lo-re - - na, Since last I held that hand in mine, And
sun's low down the sky, Lo - re - na, The frost gleams where the flow'rs have been. But the
felt the pulse beat fast, Lo - re - na, Tho' mine beat fas - ter far than thine. A

heart throbs on as warmly now, As when the summer days were nigh; Oh! the
hun-dred months, 'twas flow'ry May, When up the hil-ly slope we climbed, To.........
sun can never dip so low,.......... Adown affection's cloudless sky. The
watch the dying of the day,.......... And hear the distant church-bells chimed. To
sun can never dip so low,.......... Adown affection's cloudless sky.
watch the dying of the day,.......... And hear the distant church-bells chimed.

3. We loved each other then Lo - re - - na, More
4. The sto - ry of that past, Lo - re - - na, A-
than we ev - er dared to tell; And what we might have been, Lo - re - na, Had
- las! I care not to re - peat, The hopes that could not last, Lo - re - na, They
but our lovings prosper'd well— But then, 'tis past—the years are gone, I'll
lived, but on - ly lived to cheat. I would not cause e'en one re - gret To
not call up their shadowy forms; I'll........ say to them, "lost years, sleep on! Sleep
wran - kle in your bo - som now; For........"if we try, we may for - get,"......... Were

5.

Yes, these were words of thine, Lorena,
They burn within my memory yet;
They touched some tender chords, Lorena,
Which thrill and tremble with regret.
'Twas not thy woman's heart that spoke;
Thy heart was always true to me:—
A *duty* stern and pressing, broke
The tie which linked my soul with thee.

6.

It matters little now, Lorena,
The past—is in the eternal Past,
Our heads will soon lie low, Lorena,
Life's tide is ebbing out so fast.
There is a Future! O thank God,
Of life this is so small a part!
'Tis dust to dust beneath the sod;
But there, *up there,* 'tis heart to heart.

S. Pearson, Engr.
Chicago, Ill.

To Cousin Mary Lizzie Work,  Of New Washington, Indiana.

MARCHING THROUGH GEORGIA

SONG AND CHORUS,

In Honor of Maj. Gen. SHERMAN'S FAMOUS MARCH "from Atlanta to the Sea."

Words and Music by

HENRY CLAY WORK.

CHICAGO:

PUBLISHED BY ROOT & CADY. 67 WASHINGTON ST.

MARCHING THROUGH GEORGIA.

start the world a - long— Sing it as we used to sing it,
com - mis - sa - ry found! How the sweet po - ta - toes e - ven
had not seen for years; Hard - ly could they be re - strained from
'twas a hand - some boast, Had they not for - got, a - las! to
hun - dred to the main; Trea - son fled be - fore us, for re-
fif - ty thou - sand strong, While we were march - ing through Geor - gia.
start - ed from the ground, While we were march - ing through Geor - gia.
break - ing forth in cheers, While we were march - ing through Geor - gia.
reck - on with the host, While we were march - ing through Geor - gia.
sis - tance was in vain, While we were march - ing through Geor - gia.
CHORUS.
Air.
"Hur - rah! Hur - rah! we bring the Ju - bi - lee! Hur - rah! Hur - rah! the
Alto.
ff
Tenor.
"Hur - rah! Hur - rah! we bring the Ju - bi - lee! Hur - rah! Hur - rah! the
Base.
ff

flag that makes you free!" So we sang the cho - rus from At-
flag that makes you free!" So we sang the cho - rus from At-
lan - ta to the sea, While we were march - ing through Geor - gia.
lan - ta to the sea, While we were march - ing through Geor - gia.

MARYLAND! MY MARYLAND.

Crescite et Multiplicamini,

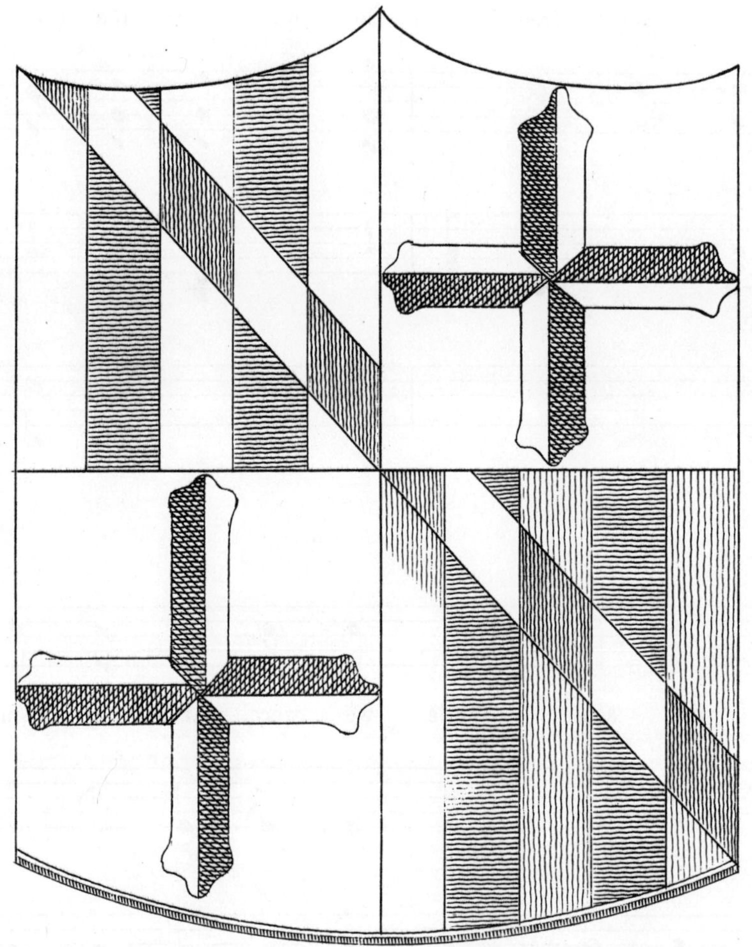

Written by

A Baltimorean in Louisianna

Music Adapted & Arranged by

Published by MILLER & BEACHAM *Baltimore.*

MARYLAND, MY MARYLAND!

-venge the pa - tri - ot - ic gore That fleck'd the streets of Bal - ti - more, And
life and death, for woe and weal, Thy peer - less chiv - al - ry re - veal, And
8va
be the Bat - tle - Queen of yore, Ma - ry - land, My Ma - ry - land!
gird thy beau - teous limbs with steel, Ma - ry - land, My Ma - ry - land!
8va

3

Thou wilt not cower in the dust,
Maryland! My Maryland!
Thy beaming sword shall never rust,
Maryland! My Maryland!
Remember Carroll's sacred trust,
Remember Howard's warlike thrust_
And all thy slumberers with the just,
Maryland! My Maryland!

4

Come! for thy shield is bright and strong,
Maryland! My Maryland!
Come! for thy dalliance, does thee wrong,
Maryland! My Maryland!
Come! to thine own heroic throng,
That stalks with Liberty along,
And give a new Key to thy song,
Maryland! My Maryland!

5

Dear Mother! burst the tyrant's chain,
Maryland! My Maryland!
Virginia should not call in vain!
Maryland! My Maryland!
She meets her sisters on the plain—
"Sic semper" tis the proud refrain,
That baffles minions back amain,
Maryland! My Maryland!

6

I see the blush upon thy cheek,
Maryland! My Maryland!
But thou wast ever bravely meek,
Maryland! My Maryland!
But lo! there surges forth a shriek
From hill to hill, from creek to creek—
Potomac calls to Chesapeake,
Maryland! My Maryland!

7

Thou wilt not yield the vandal toll,
Maryland! My Maryland!
Thou wilt not crook to his control,
Maryland! My Maryland!
Better the fire upon thee roll,
Better the blade, the shot, the bowl,
Than crucifixion of the soul,
Maryland! My Maryland!

8

I hear the distant thunder-hum,
Maryland! My Maryland!
The Old Line's bugle, fife and drum,
Maryland! My Maryland!
She is not dead, nor deaf, nor dumb—
Huzza! she spurns the Northern scum!
She breathes_ she burns! she'll come! she'll come!
Maryland! My Maryland!

25 cts nett.

NEW YORK

Published by FIRTH, POND & CO. *1 Franklin Square,*

Pittsburgh,	*Cleveland,*	*St. Louis.*
H. KLEBER.	HOLBROOK & LONG.	BALMER & WEBER.

MY OLD KENTUCKY HOME, GOOD-NIGHT!

Words and Music by

STEPHEN C. FOSTER.

corn top's ripe and the meadow's in the bloom While the birds make music all the
day. The young folks roll on the lit_tle cabin floor, All
merry, all happy and bright: By'n by Hard Times comes a
knocking at the door, Then my old Kentucky Home, good night!

CHORUS

Tenor.
Weep no more, my lady, oh! weep no more to_ day! We will sing one song For the
AIR.
1st Soprano.
2d Soprano.
Weep no more, my lady, oh! weep no more to_ day! We will sing one song For the
Bass.
old Kentucky Home, For the old Kentucky Home, far a_ way.
old Kentucky Home, For the old Kentucky Home, far a_ way.

2d. V.
They hunt no more for the possum and the coon On the meadow, the hill and the shore, They
sing no more by the glimmer of the moon, On the bench by the old cabin door. The
day goes by like a shadow o'er the heart, With sorrow where all was de_light: The
time has come when the darkies have to part, Then my old Kentucky Home, good-night! Chorus.
3d. V.
The head must bow and the back will have to bend, Wherever the darkey may go: A
few more days, and the trouble all will end In the field where the sugar-canes grow. A
few more days for to tote the weary load, No matter 'twill never be light, A
few more days till we totter on the road, Then my old Kentucky Home, good-night! Chorus.
Quidor Engvr.

NEW AND IMPROVED EDITION.

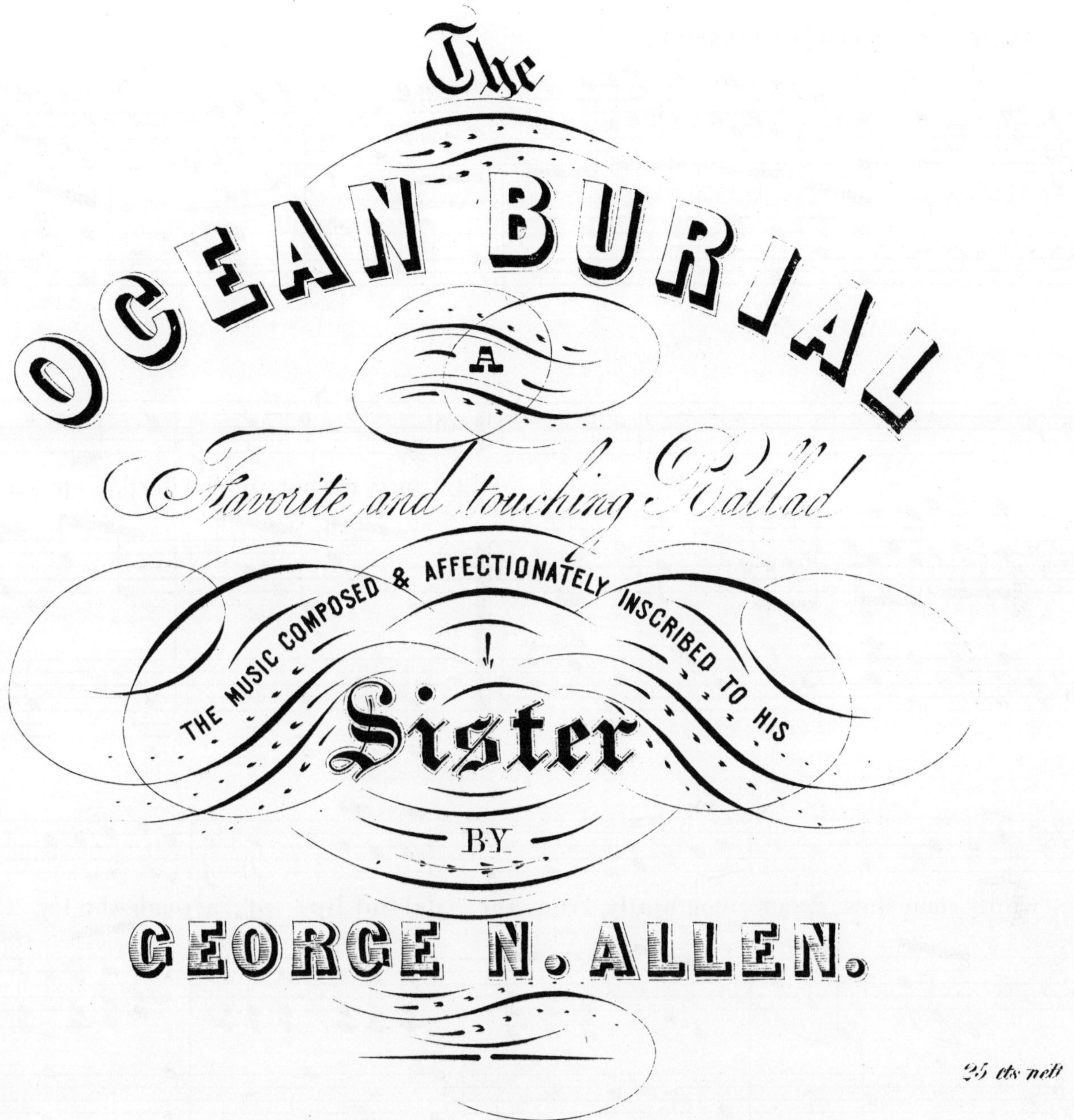

BOSTON *Published by* OLIVER DITSON *115 Washington st.*

THE OCEAN BURIAL.

MODERATE WITH EXPRESSION.

death-shade had slow - ly passed, and now, Where the land and his fond loved
Ritard
home were nigh, They had gathered around him to see him die.
Ritard
O bu - ry me not in the
deep, deep sea, Where the billowy shroud will roll over me, Where no

light will break through the dark, cold wave, And no sun-beam rest up-
on my grave. It mat-ters not, I have oft been told, Where the
bo-dy shall lie when the heart is cold, Yet grant ye O! grant ye this
boon to me, O! bu-ry me not in the deep, deep sea."
Ritard:
Ritard:

3

"For in fancy I've listened to the well known words,
The free, wild winds, and the songs of the birds;
I have thought of home, of cot and bower,
And of scenes that I loved in childhood's hour.
I had ever hoped to be laid when I died,
In the church-yard there, on the green hill-side;
By the bones of my fathers' my grave should be,
O! bury me not in the deep, deep sea.

4

"Let my death slumbers be where a mother's prayer,
And a sister's tear shall be mingled there;
O! 'twill be sweet, ere the heart's throb is o'er,
To know when its fountains shall gush no more,
That those it so fondly hath yearned for will come
To plant the first wild-flower of spring on my tomb;
Let me lie where those loved ones will weep over me,
O! bury me not in the deep, deep sea.

5

"And there is another; her tears would be shed,
For him who lay far in an ocean bed;
In hours that it pains me to think of now,
She hath twined these locks, and hath kissed this brow.
In the hair she hath wreathed, shall the sea snake hiss?
And the brow she hath pressed, shall the cold wave kiss?
For the sake of that bright one that waiteth for me,
O! bury me not in the deep, deep sea.

6

"She hath been in my dreams"— his voice failed there;
They gave no heed to his dying prayer;
They have lowered him slow o'er the vessel's side,
Above him has closed the dark, cold tide;
Where to dip their light wings the sea-fowls rest
Where the blue waves dance o'er the ocean's crest;
Where the billows bound, and the winds sport free;
They have buried him there, in the deep, deep sea.

1. **Carry Me Back to Old Virginny.** (Song & Chorus.) 4

2. **In the Morning by the Bright Light.** (End Song.) 4

3 **Oh dem Golden Slippers.** (Song & Chorus.) 4

Words and Music by JAMES BLAND, of Sprague's Georgia Minstrels.

BOSTON:

JOHN F. PERRY & Co., Music Publishers.

OH, DEM GOLDEN SLIPPERS!

long, white robe dat I bought last June, I'm gwine to git changed Kase it fits too soon, And de
Brud-der Ben and Sis-ter Luce, Dey will tel-e-graph de news to Un-cle Bac-co Juice, What a
gold-en slippers must be nice and clean, And yer age must be Just sweet six-teen, And yer
ole grey hoss dat I used to drive, I will hitch him to de char-iot in de morn.
great camp-meetin' der will be dat day, When we ride up in de char-iot in de morn.
white kid gloves yer will have to wear, When yer ride up in de char-iot in de morn.
8va
fz
CHORUS.
Soprano.
(First time pp, repeat ff.)
Oh, dem golden slippers! Oh, dem golden slippers! Golden slippers I'm gwine to wear, be-case dey look so
Alto.
Tenor.
Oh, dem golden slippers! Oh, dem golden slippers! Golden slippers I'm gwine to wear, be-case dey look so
Bass.
(First time pp, repeat ff.)

neat;
Oh, dem golden slippers! Oh, dem golden slippers! Golden slippers Ise gwine to wear, To
neat;
Oh, dem golden slippers! Oh, dem golden slippers! Golden slippers Ise gwine to wear, To
1st.
2d.
walk de golden street.... street.
walk de golden street.... street.
1st.
2d.
f
fz

OH MY DARLING
CLEMENTINE
WORDS & MUSIC BY
PERCY MONTROSE.
3
BOSTON.
Copyright 1884 by
OLIVER DITSON & CO. 451 WASHINGTON ST.
N.YORK, C.H.DITSON & CO.
CHICAGO, LYON & HEALY.
PHILA. J.E.DITSON & CO.
St. Louis, J.L. Peters.
Galveston, T. Goggan & Bro.
S. Francisco, Sherman, Clay & Co

OH MY DARLING CLEMENTINE.

Song and Chorus.

Words and Music **by Percy Montrose.**

1. In a cab - in, In a can - on, an ex - ca - va - tion for a
2. She drove her ducklets, To the riv - er, Ev'ry morning just at
3. I saw her lips a - bove the wa - ter, Blowing bub - bles soft and
mine; Dwelt a mi - ner, A For - ty - ni - ner, And his daughter Cle - men - tine.
nine; She stubb'd her toe, a - gainst a sliv - er, And - fell in - to the foam-ing brine.
fine; A - las for me, I was no swimmer, And so I lost my Cle - men - tine.
CHORUS.
Sopr:
Oh my dar - ling, Oh my dar - ling, Oh my dar - ling Cle - men - tine, You are
Alto.
Cle - men - tine, Clementine, Clemen - Cle - men - tine, Clemen - Clemen -
Tenor.
Cle - men - tine, Clementine, Clemen - Cle - men - tine, Clemen - Clemen -
Bass.
Oh Cle - men - tine, Oh Clementine, Oh Clemen Cle - men - tine, Clemen - Clemen -
Piano.
mf

lost and gone for - ev - er, Dref - ful sor - ry, Cle - men - tine.
tine, Cle-men-tine, Cle-men-tine, Clemen - Cle - men - tine.
tine, Cle-men-tine, Cle-men-tine, Clemen - Cle - men - tine.
tine, Cle-men-tine, Oh Cle-men-tine, Oh Clemen - Cle - men - tine.
Interlude.

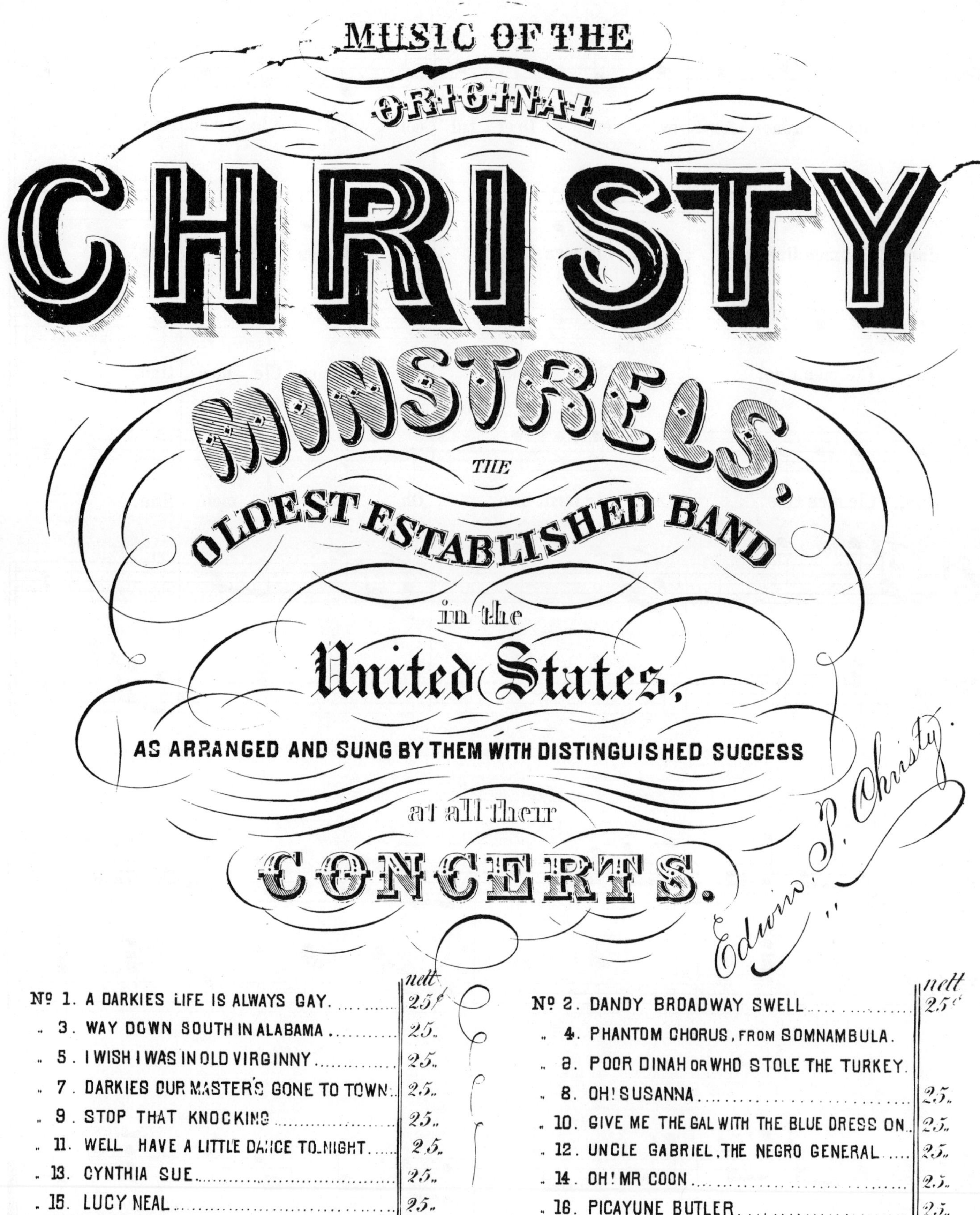

NEW YORK.

Published by C. HOLT Jr. *156 Fulton St.*

BOSTON: OLIVER DITSON.

OH! SUSANNA.

Sung by
G. N. CHRISTY,
Of the
CHRISTY MINSTRELS.
ALLEGRETTO.
p
f
I came from Al_a_ba_ma wid my
ban_jo on my knee, I'm g'wan to Lou_si_a_na My
true love for to see, It rain'd all night the day I left, The

weather it was dry, The sun so hot I
frose to death; Sus-an-na, dont you cry.
CHORUS.
1st Voice.
Oh! Sus-an-na, Oh! dont you cry for me, I've
2nd Voice.
Oh! Sus-an-na, Oh! dont you cry for me, I've
TENOR
Oh! Sus-an-na, Oh! dont you cry for me, I've
BASS
Oh! Sus-an-na Oh! dont you cry for me, I've
PIANO
FORTE

2

I jumped aboard de telegraph,
And trabbelled down de riber,
De Lectric fluid magnified,
And killed five hundred Nigger
De bullgine bust, de horse run off,
I realy thought I'd die;
I shut my eyes to hold my breath,
Susanna, dont you cry.
Oh! Susanna - etc.

3

I had a dream de odder night
When ebery ting was still;
I thought I saw Susanna,
A coming down de hill.
The buckwheat cake war in her mouth,
The tear was in her eye,
Says I'm coming from de South,
Susanna, dont you cry.
Oh! Susanna - etc.

4

I soon will be in New Orleans,
And den I'll look all round,
And when I find Susanna,
I'll fall upon the ground.
But if I do not find her,
Dis darkie 'I surely die,
And when I'm dead and buried,
Susanna, dont you cry.
Oh! Susanna - etc.

Foster's Melodies

Nº. 49.

OLD BLACK JOE

SONG

Written and Composed by

STEPHEN C. FOSTER.

Author of

FAIRY BELLE, GLENDY BURK &C.

2½

NEW YORK
Published by FIRTH, POND & CO. 547 Broadway.

Boston.
O. DITSON & CO.

Cincinnati.
C. Y. FONDA.

Pittsburgh.
H KLEBER & BRO

OLD BLACK JOE.

CHORUS.
I'm coming, I'm coming, for my head is bending low: I
I'm com - ing, I'm com - ing, for my head is bending low: I
hear those gen - - tle voi - - ces call - - ing, "Old Black Joe."
hear those gen - - tle voi - - ces call - - ing, "Old Black Joe."

II. VERSE. Why do I weep when my heart should feel no pain
III. VERSE. Where are the hearts once so hap - py and so free? The
Why do I sigh that my friends come not a - gain,
chil - - dren so dear that I held up - on my knee,
Griev - ing for forms Now de - par - ted long a - go? I
Gone to the shore where my soul has longed to go. I
hear their gen - tle voi - ces call - ing "Old Black Joe."
hear their gen - tle voi - ces call - ing "Old Black Joe."

OLD DAN EMMIT'S
ORIGINAL BANJO MELODIES
EMMIT, BROWER, WHITLOCK, PELHAM
On Stone by W. Sharp from a sketch by Johnston
As sung by the VIRGINIA MINSTRELS with enthusiastic applause at the principal Theatres and Concerts in the Union, being an entire new collection of peices, never before Published.
O DANCE DE BOATMAN DANCE
TWILL NEBBER DO TO GIB IT UP SO
OLD DAN TUCKER
I'M GWINE OBER DE MOUNTAINS
THE FINE OLD COLORED GENTLEMAN
MY OLD AUNT SALLY
O LUD GALS GIB US &C
PRICE, EACH 25 CTS. nett
BOUVÉ & SHARP Lith.rs Boston
Arranged for the Piano Forte by
RICE.
BOSTON.
Published by CHAS. H. KEITH 67 & 69 Court St.
Entered according to act of Congress in the year 1843 by Chas H. Keith in the clerks office of the district Court of Massachusetts.

The Original

OLD DAN TUCKER.

As sung by the Virginia Minstrels.

Words by Old Dan. D. Emmit.

Boston: Published by C. H. Keith, 67 & 69 Court St.

2

Tucker is a nice old man,
He use to ride our darby ram;
He sent him whizzen down de hill,
If he had'nt got up he'd lay dar still.
Get out, &c.

3

Here's my razor in good order
Magnum bonum—jis hab bought 'er;
Sheep shell oats, Tucker shell de corn,
I'll shabe you soon as de water get warm.
Get out &c.

4

Ole Dan Tucker an I got drunk,
He fell in de fire an kick up a chunk,
De charcoal got inside he shoe
Lor bless you honey how de ashes flew.
Get out &c.

5

Down de road foremost de stump,
Massa make me work de pump;
I pump so hard I broke de sucker,
Dar was work for ole Dan Tucker.
Get out, &c.

6

I went to town to buy some goods
I lost myself in a piece of woods,
De night was dark I had to suffer,
It froze de heel of Daniel Tucker.
Get out &c.

7

Tucker was a hardened sinner,
He nebber said his grace at dinner;
De ole sow squeel, de pigs did squall
He 'hole hog wid de tail and all.
Get out &c.

OLD FOLKS AT HOME
ETHIOPIAN MELODY
As Sung by
Christy's Minstrels
WRITTEN AND COMPOSED BY
E. P. CHRISTY.
Weller & Greene
25 ¢ nett.
NEW YORK Published by FIRTH. POND & CO. 1 Franklin Sq.
PITTSBURG. H. KLEBER.

OLD FOLKS AT HOME

Words and Music by E. P. CHRISTY.

All up and down de whole cre_ation, Sad_ _ _ly I roam,
Still longing for de old plan_ta_tion, And for de old folks at home.
CHORUS.
All de world am sad and dreary, Eb_ry where I roam,
Oh! darkeys how my heart grows weary, Far from de old folks at home.

2d. VERSE.
All round de little farm I wandered When I was young,
Den many happy days I squandered, Many de songs I sung.
When I was playing wid my brudder Hap---py was I ---
Oh! take me to my kind old mudder, Dere let me live and die. CHORUS.
3d. VERSE.
One lit-tle hut a-mong de bushes, One dat I love,
Still sad-ly to my mem'ry rushes, No matter where I rove
When will I see de bees a humming All round de comb?
When will I hear de banjo tumming Down in my good old home? CHORUS.
Quidor Engvr.

SCOTCH AIR

Words by WOODWORTH. 3½ Music by KIALLMARK.

BOSTON.
Published by OLIVER DITSON & CO. 451 Washington St.
NEW YORK. C.H. DITSON & CO. CHICAGO. LYON & HEALY. SAN FRANCISCO. SHERMAN, HYDE & CO. PHILADELPHIA. J.E. DITSON & CO.
F.M. HASKELL & CO. LITH. 61 HANOVER ST. BOSTON.

THE OLD OAKEN BUCKET.

KIALLMARK.

The wide - spreading stream, the
How ar - dent I seized it with
And now far removed from the
p
mill that stood near it, The bridge and the rock where the cat - a - ract fell; The
hands that were glow-ing, And quick to the white - pebbled bot - tom it fell; Then
loved sit - u - a - tion, The tear of re - gret will in - stru - sive - ly swell; As
cot of my fa - ther, the dai -ry house by it, And e'en the rude buck - et that hung in the well.
soon with the em - blem of health o - ver-flowing, And dripping with cool - ness it rose from the well.
fan - cy re - verts to my father's, plan-ta-tion, And sighs for the buck - et that hung in the well.

CHORUS.
SOPRANO.
The old oak-en buck-et, the i-ron-bound buck-et, The moss-cover'd buck-et that
ALTO.
TENOR.
The old oak-en buck-et, the i-ron-bound buck-et, The moss-cover'd buck-et that
BASS.
rit.
hung in the well.
rit.
hung in the well.
rit.
rit.
p
sf
smorz.
pp.

Lith. of Wild & Chevalier, 72 Dock St. Phil.

OLD ROSIN THE BEAU

Favourite Comic Song

Dedicated with much respect

to the members of the

FALCON BARGE

by the Publisher.

Arranged by

J. C. BECKELL.

Price 25 cts. nett.

PHILADELPHIA,

Osbourn's Music Saloon 30 S. 4th St.

ROSIN THE BOW.

I've always been cheerful and easy,
And scarce have I heeded a foe,
While some after money run crazy,
I merrily Rosin'd the Bow.

Some youngsters were panting for fashions,
Some new kick seemed now all the go,
But having no turbulent passions,
My motto was "Rosin the Bow."

So kindly my parents besought me,
No longer a roving to go,
And friends whom I thought had forgot me,
With gladness met Rosin the Bow.

My young days I spent all in roving,
But never was vicious, no, no;
But somehow I loved to keep moving,
And cheerfully Rosin'd the Bow.

In country or city, no matter,
Too often I never could go,
My presence all sadness would scatter,
So cheerful was Robin the Bow.

The old people always grew merry,
Young faces with pleasure did glow,
While lips with the red of cherry,
Sipped "bliss to old Rosin the Bow."

While sweetly I played on my viol,
In measures so soft and so slow,
Old Time stopped the shade on the dial,
To listen to Rosin the Bow.

And tho my sweet prime I've been spending,
When friendship made glasses ere now,
No pang of remorse is now rending,
The bosom of Rosin the Bow.

And peacefully now I am sinking,
From all this sweet world can bestow,
But Heaven's kind mercy I'm thinking,
Provides for old Rosin the Bow.

Now soon some still Sunday morning,
The first thing the neighbors will know,
Their ears will be met with the warning,
To bury old Rosin the Bow.

My friends will then so neatly dress me,
In linen as white as the snow,
And in my new coffin they'll press me,
And whisper "poor Rosin the Bow."

Then lone with my head on the pillow,
In peace I'll be sleeping below,
The grass and the breeze shaken willow,
That waves over Rosin the Bow.

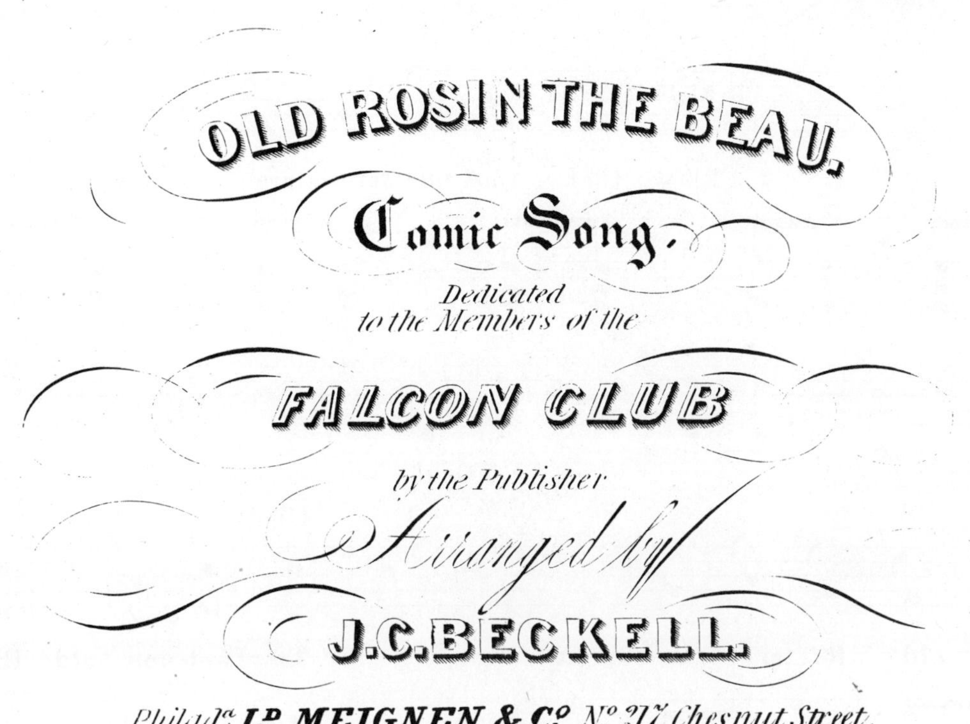

OLD ROSIN THE BEAU.

Comic Song.

Dedicated
to the Members of the

FALCON CLUB

by the Publisher

Arranged by

J.C.BECKELL.

*Philad*a. **L.P MEIGNEN & C.o** *N.o 217 Chesnut Street.*

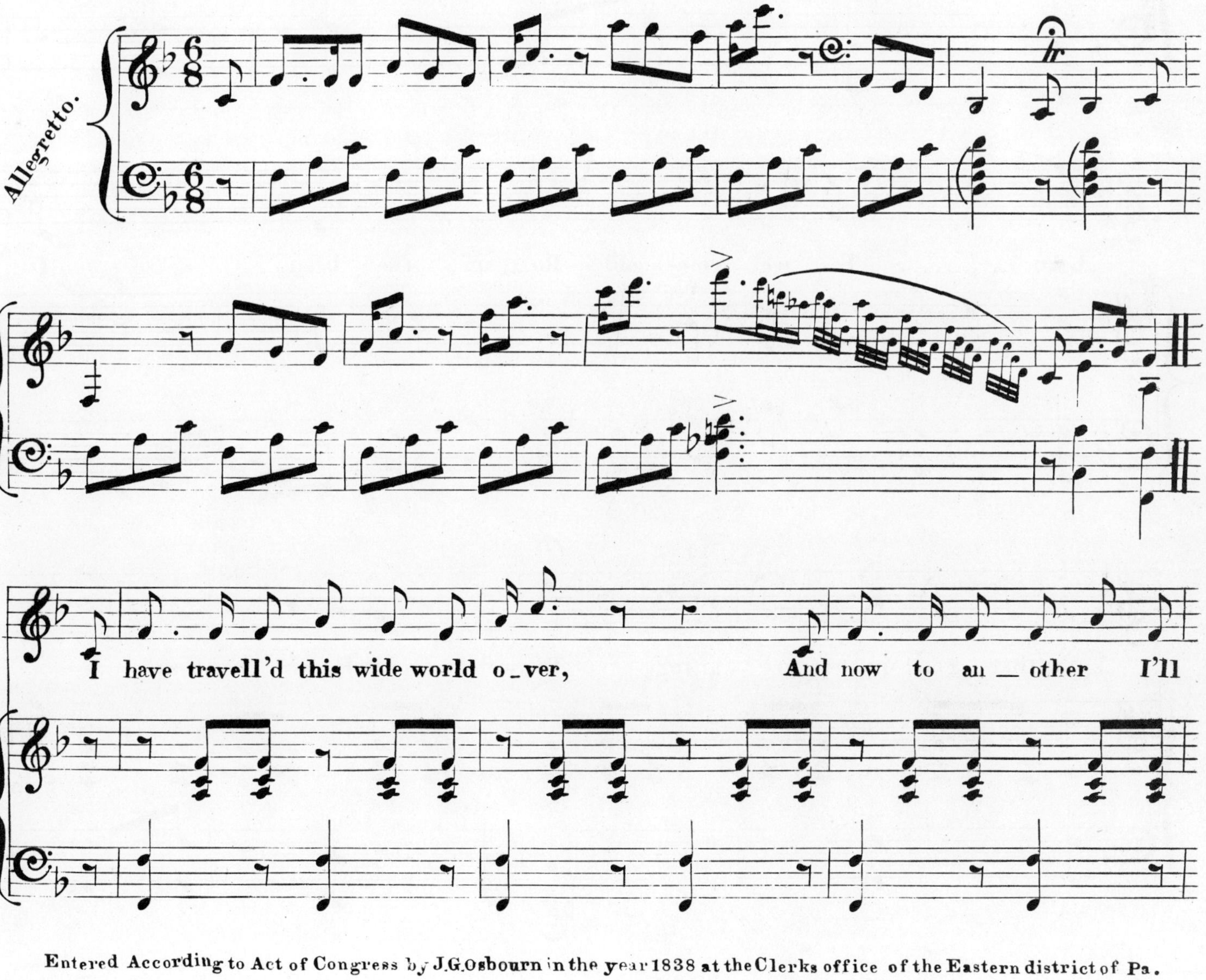
Allegretto.
I have travell'd this wide world o_ver, And now to an_other I'll

go, I know that good quarters are wai_ting To
Chorus.
welcome old Ro_sin the beau To welcome old Ro_sin the
beau............ To wel_come old Ro_sin the beau I
know that good quarters are waiting, To welcome old Ro_sin the beau
Sym

2.

When I'm dead and laid out on the counter,
A voice you will hear from below
Singing some plain whiskey and water
To drink to old Rosin the beau.
To drink &c.

3.

And when I am dead I reckon
The ladies will all want to know
Just lift the lid off of the coffin
And look at old Rosin the beau.
And look &c.

4.

I'll have to be buried I'm thinking
And I would like it done just so
And be sure not to go contrary
To the wish of old Rosin the beau.
To the &c.

5.

You must get some dozen good fellows
And stand them all round in a row
And drink out of half gallon bottles
To the name of old Rosin the beau.
To the &c.

6.

Get four or five jovial young fellows
And let them all staggering go
And dig a deep hole in the meadow
And in it toss Rosin the beau.
And in it &c.

7.

Then get you a couple of donecks
Place one at my head and my toe
And do not fail to scratch on it
The name of old Rosin the beau.
The name &c.

8.

I feel the grim tyrant approaching
That cruel implacable foe,
Who spares neither age or condition
Nor even old Rosin the beau.
Nor even &c.

Pop Goes the Weazel
Song
Arranged by
Chas. Twiggs Esq.
New York.
Published by Stephen T. Gordon, 297 Broadway.
Philad.
John E Gould.
Boston
Oliver Ditson.
New Orleans
Horatio D. Hewitt.
Cincinnati.
Curtiss & Truax.

POP GOES DE WEASEL.

Arranged by CHARLEY TWIGGS

CHORUS.
"Pop goes de Wea -- -- sel." Oh all de dance dat
eb -- ber was plann'd To gal -- -- vanize de heel and de hand, Dar's
CHORUS.
none dat moves so gay and grand As "Pop goes de
Wea -- -- sel." De lov -- -- -- er, when he pants t'rough fear, To

2.

John Bull tells, in de ole cow's hum,
How Uncle Sam used *Uncle Tom,*
While he makes some white folks *slaves* at home,
By "Pop goes de Weasel!"
He talks about a friendly trip
To Cuba in a steam war-ship,
But Uncle Sam may make him skip
By "Pop goes dee Weasel!"
He's sending forth his iron hounds
To bark us off de fishin' grounds—
He'd best beware of Freedom's sounds
Oh "Pop goes de Weasel!"

3.

De Temperance folks from Souf to Main,
Against all liquor spout and strain,
But when dey feels an ugly pain
Den "Pop goes de Weasel!"
All New York in rush now whirls
Whar de *World's Fair* its flag unfurls,
But de best World's Fair am when our girls
Dance "Pop goes de Weasel!"
Den form two lines as straight as a string,
Dance in and out, den three in a ring—
Dive under like de duck, and sing
"Pop goes de Weasel!"

Pearson.

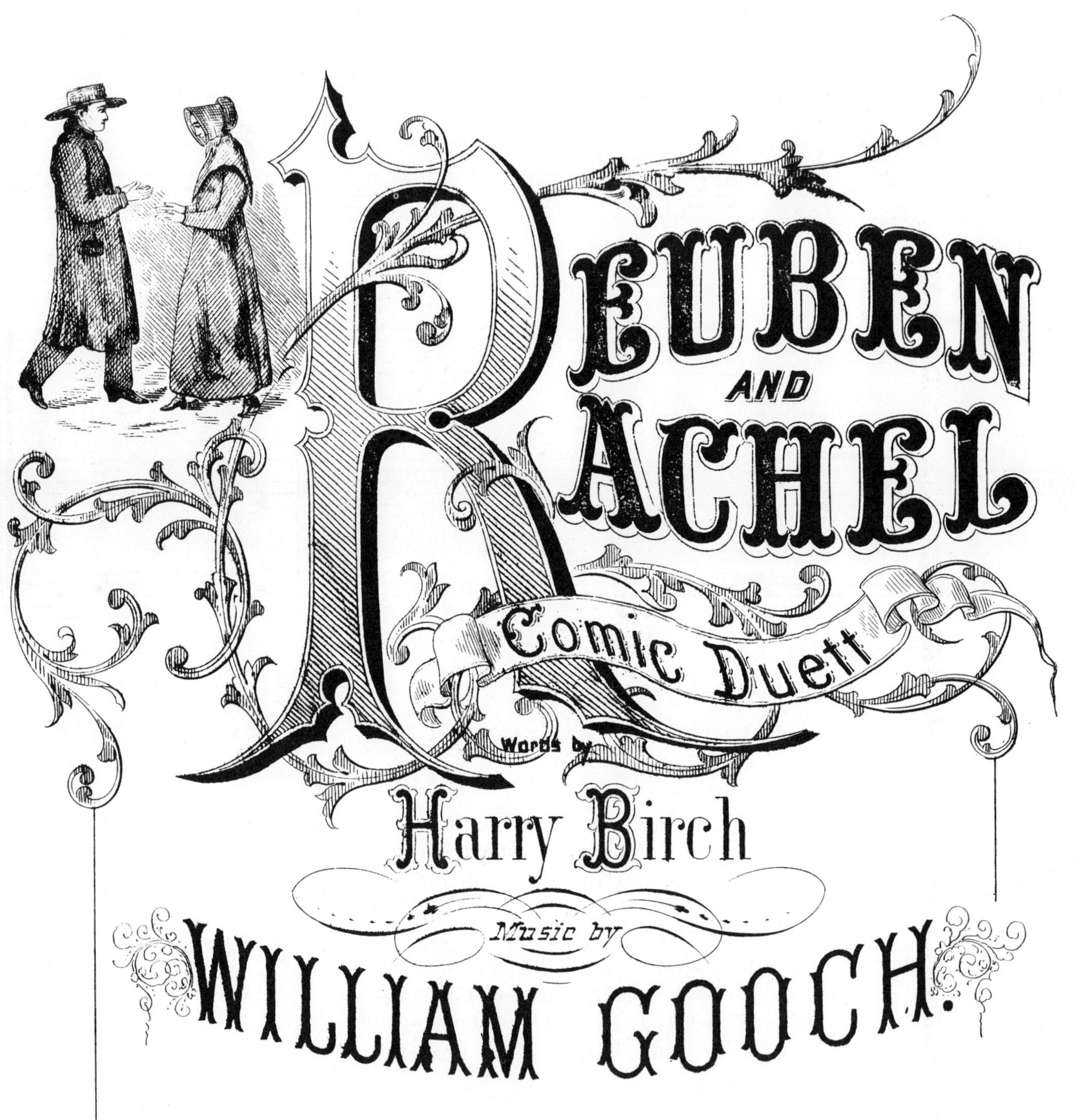

3½

BOSTON
WHITE, SMITH & PERRY
298, 300 Washington St
Root & Cady. Chicago. Wm. A. Pond & Co. N. York. Lee & Walker. Phila

REUBEN AND RACHEL.

Words by ***HARRY BIRCH.*** *Music by* ***WILLIAM GOOCH.***

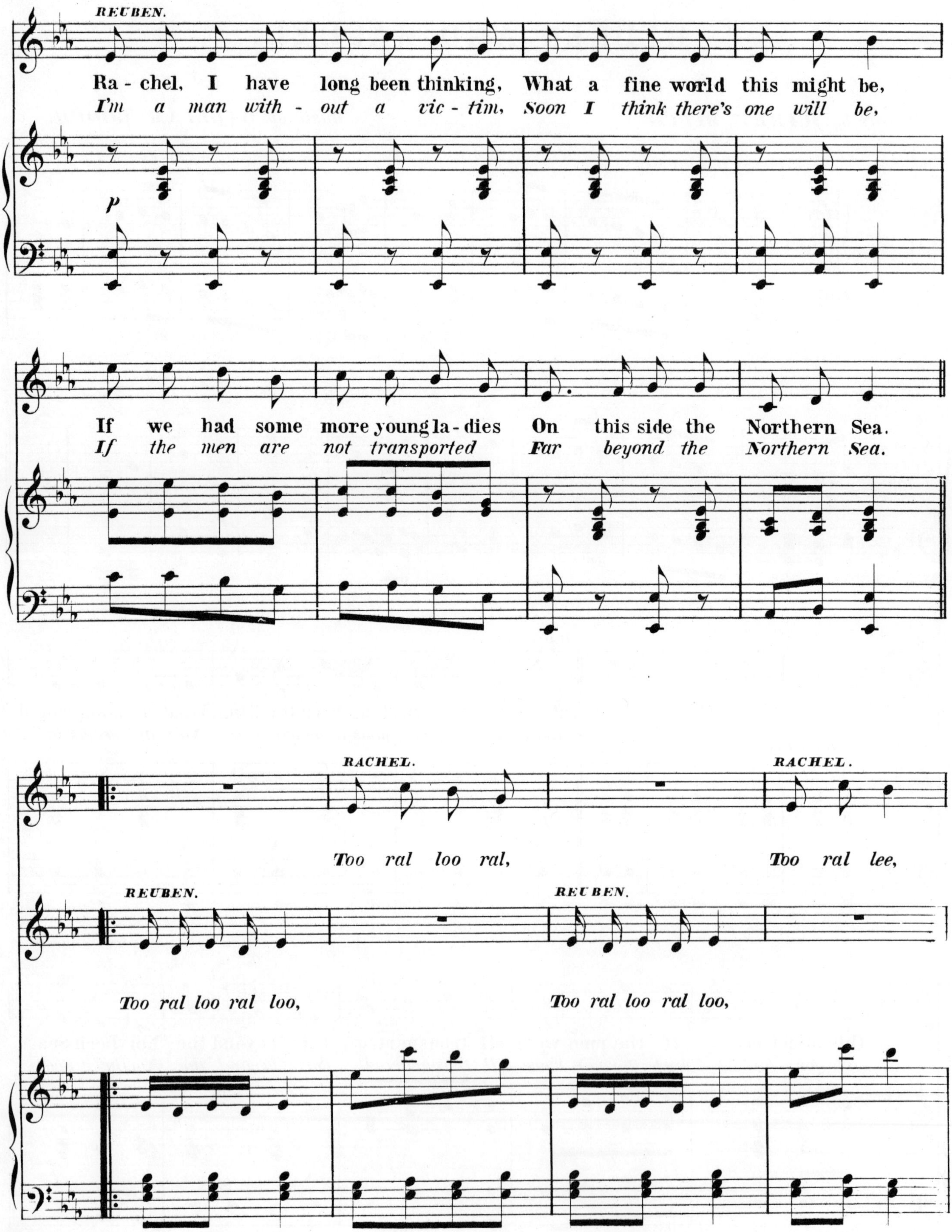

REUBEN.

Ra - chel, I have long been thinking, What a fine world this might be,
I'm a man with - out a vic - tim, Soon I think there's one will be,

p

If we had some more young la - dies On this side the Northern Sea.
If the men are not transported Far beyond the Northern Sea.

3.

RACH. Reuben, what's the use of fooling,
Why not come up like a man?
If you'd like to have a "lovyer"
I'm for life your "Sally Ann."

REU. Oh my goodness! oh my gracious!
What a queer world this would be,
If the men were all transported
Far beyond the Northern Sea!

4.

RACH. Reuben, now do stop your teazing,
If you've any love for me;
I was only just a fooling,
As I thought of course you'd see.

REU. Rachel, I will not transport you,
But will take you for a wife,
We will live on "milk and honey,"
Better or worse, we're in for life.

Rocked in the Cradle of the Deep.

SUNG BY

MR. BRAHAM.

THE WORDS BY

MRS. WILLARD.

(Of Troy)

THE MUSIC

Composed and respectfully Dedicated to

Dr. Mitchell

BY

J. P. Knight.

Pr. 38 C. nett

A. BARBER Sc.

New York. Published by C.E. HORN, 367 Broadway.

Where may be had by the same Composer

CUPID 'MID THE ROSES PLAYING.	THE NEW YEARS COME.
IN THE DAYS WHEN WE WENT GIPSYING.	THE GRECIAN DAUGHTER &c.&c.

ROCK'D IN THE CRADLE OF THE DEEP
The Words by Mrs Willard of Troy
The Music by J.P. Knight.
Copy Right Secured
Rock'd in the cradle of the deep...... I lay me down in peace to sleep; Se---

- - cure I rest up - on the wave........... For thou Oh! Lord, hast
power to save. I know thou wilt not slight my
call, For thou dost mark the sparrow's fall! And
calm and peace - ful is my sleep..................... Rock'd in the

pp
cra - dle of the deep, And calm and peace - - ful is my
tr
tr
pp
sleep ...... Rock'd in the cra - - dle of the deep.
tr
tr
tr
mf
pp
tr
tr
Ped:
dim
And such the trust that still were mine ...... Tho' stor - my

ff
winds swept o'er the brine Or tho' the tem - pest's fie - - ry
ff
p
breath Rous'd me from sleep to wreck and death! In
o - - - - - cean cave still safe with Thee, The germ of
im - - mor - - ta - - - - li - - - - ty ; And calm and peace - ful is my

pp
sleep .... Rock'd in the cra_-dle of the deep, And
calm and peace_-ful is my sleep ..... Rock'd in the
cra_-dle of the deep.
mf
Ped:

To

J. C. Trowbridge Esq

SHEW FLY DONT BOTHER ME

Comic Song and Dance

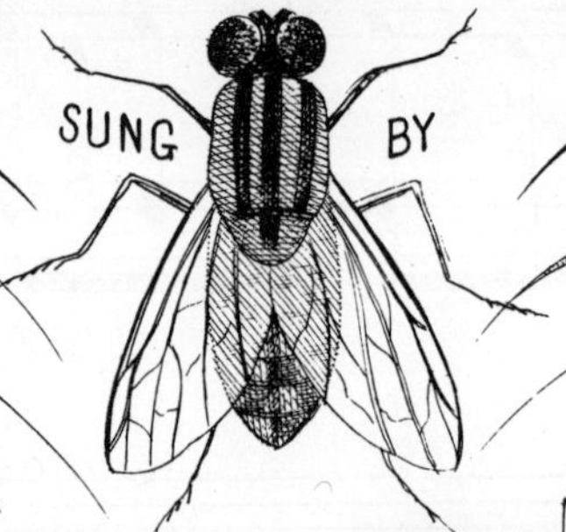

SUNG BY

Cool Burgess, and Rollin Howard,

MELODY BY
FRANK CAMPBELL,
ARRANGED BY
ROLLIN HOWARD.

3½

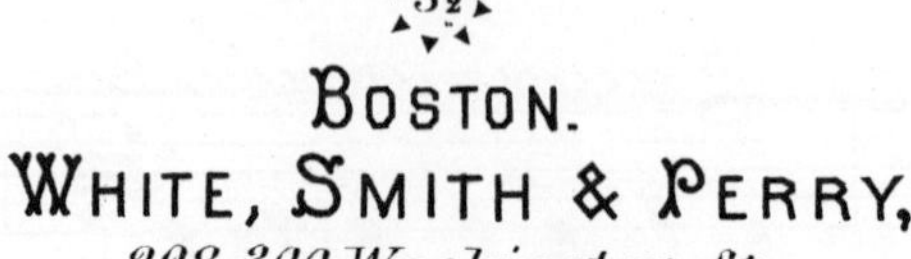

BOSTON.
WHITE, SMITH & PERRY,
298, 300 Washington St.

Prov. R. I.
CORY BROS.

St. Johnsbury, Vt.
L. B. HARRINGTON SONS & CO.

N. YORK J. L. PETERS.

SHEW! FLY, DON'T BOTHER ME.

COMIC SONG AND DANCE.
OR
WALK ROUND.

Words by BILLY REEVES. *arr: by* ROLLIN HOWARD.

feel, I feel, I feel, That's what my moth-er said, The
feel I feel I feel, That's what my moth-er said, When-
an-gels pour-ing 'las-ses down, Up-on this nig-ger's head.
ev-er this nig-ger goes to sleep, He must cover up his head.
CHORUS.
Shew! fly, don't both-er me, Shew! fly, don't both-er me,
Shew! fly, don't both-er me, I belong to comp'-ny G. I

feel, I feel, I feel, I feel like a morning star, I feel, I feel, I
feel, I feel like a morning star. I feel, I feel, I feel, I
feel like a morning star, I feel, I feel I, feel, I feel like a morning star.

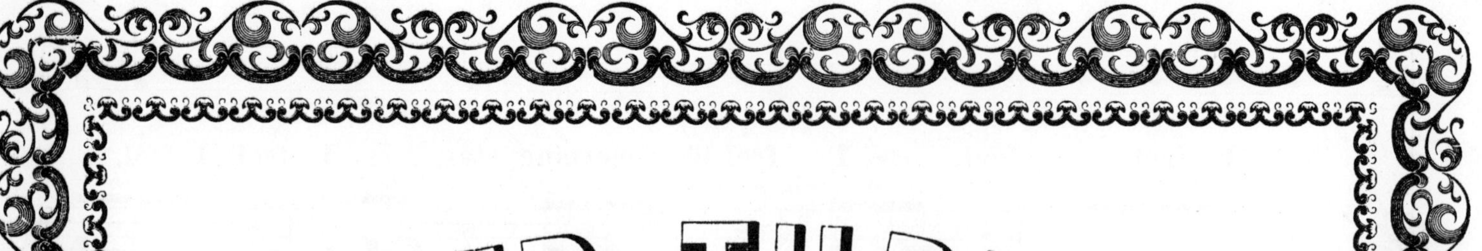

AMONG THE GOLD.

SONG AND CHORUS.

WORDS BY EBEN E. REXFORD, MUSIC BY

H. P. DANKS,

AUTHOR OF

THE GREAT POPULAR SONG,

DON'T BE ANGRY WITH ME, DARLING.

Song and Chorus, Keys F and G, Price, 35 Cts. each.

Don't You think so, Kitty?
Song and Chorus, Key B flat.

Let the Angels in.
Song and Chorus, Key E flat.

Beautiful form of my Dreams.
Ballad, Key C.

Why so sad, my Precious Darling?
Song and Chorus, Key G.

Sleep my Dear One.
Song and Chorus, Key C.

Bring me a Pretty Bouquet.
Ballad, Key C.

Each, 35 Cents.

CHARLES W. HARRIS,
New York, 750 Broadway.
Troy, N. Y., 265 River St.

3½

Taylor & Barwood, Music Stereotypers, Rose Street, N. Y.

SILVER THREADS AMONG THE GOLD.

SONG AND CHORUS.

Words by EBEN. E REXFORD. *Music by H. P. DANKS.*

But my darling, you will be, will be— Al - ways young and fair to me,—
Oh! my darling, mine a - lone, a - lone— You have nev - er old - er grown,—
rall.
Yes! my dar - ling, you will be...... Al - ways young and fair to me.
Yes! my dar - ling, mine a - lone...... You have nev - er old - er grown!
rall.
CHORUS.
SOPRANO.
Dar - ling, I am growing, grow - ing old, Sil - ver threads among the gold,
ALTO.
Dar - ling, I am grow - ing old, Sil - ver threads a - mong the gold,
TENOR.
Dar - ling, I am grow - ing old, Sil - ver threads a - mong the gold,
BASS.

3.

Love can never more grow old,
Locks may lose their brown and gold;
Cheeks may fade and hollow grow,
But the hearts that love will know
Never, never winter's frost and chill:
Summer warmth is in them still—
Never winter's frost and chill,
Summer warmth is in them still.—*Cho.*

4.

Love is always young and fair,—
What to us is silver hair,
Faded cheeks, or steps grown slow,
To the heart that beats below?
Since I kissed you mine alone, alone,
You have never older grown—
Since I kissed you mine alone,
You have never older grown.—*Cho.*

BOSTON.
Published by OLIVER DITSON & CO. 451 Washington St.

NEW YORK
G.H.DITSON & CO
711 BROADWAY.

CHICAGO
LYON&HEALY.

BOSTON
J.C.HAYNES & CO.

PHILA.
J.E.DITSON &CO.
SUCCESSORS TO LEE &WALKER.

J.H. BUFFORD'S SONS LITH. 141 FRANKLIN ST. BOSTON.

SWEET BY AND BY.

Words by S. Fillmore Bennett. *Music by J. P. Webster.*

way, To pre - pare us a dwell - ing - place there.
more— Not a sigh for the bless - ing of rest.
love, And the bless - ing that hal - - low our days!
CHORUS.
In the sweet by and by, We shall
In the sweet by and by, We shall
In the sweet by and by, In the sweet by and by, We shall
by and by, by and by, We shall

In the repeat diminuendo gradually to the end.
meet on that beau - - ti - ful shore, In the sweet by and
meet on that beau - - ti - ful shore, In the sweet by and
meet on that beau - - ti - ful shore, by and by, In the sweet by and by, In the
meet on that beau - - ti - ful shore, by and by, by and by,
by, We shall meet on that beau - ti - ful shore.
by, We shall meet on that beau - ti - ful shore.
sweet by and by, We shall meet on that beau - ti - ful shore.
By and by we shall meet on that beau - ti - ful shore.

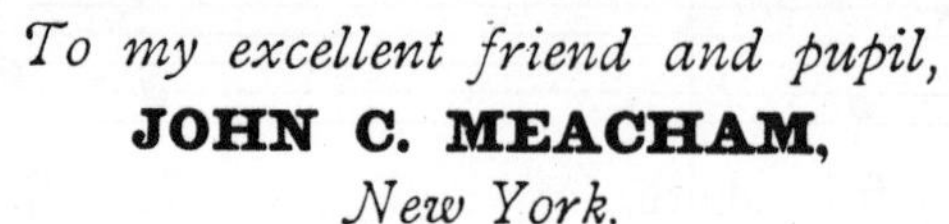

To my excellent friend and pupil,
JOHN C. MEACHAM,
New York.

Sweet Genevieve.

Song and Chorus.

Words by
GEORGE COOPER.

MUSIC BY
HENRY TUCKER.

3

New York:
WM. A. POND & CO.,
547 Broadway and 39 Union Square.

Milwaukee:	*San Francisco:*	*Boston:*	*Cincinnati, O.:*	*New Orleans:*
H. N. HEMPSTED.	M. GRAY.	WHITE & GOULLAUD.	C. Y. FONDA.	L. GRUNEWALD.

SWEET GENEVIEVE.

(SONG AND CHORUS.)

Words by GEORGE COOPER. Music by HENRY TUCKER.

rose of youth was dew - impearled; But now it with - ers in the blast. I
heart shall nev - er, nev - er rove: Thou art my on - ly guid - ing star. For
see thy face in ev - 'ry dream, My wak - ing thoughts are full of thee; Thy
me the past has no re - gret What - e'er the years may bring to me; I
glance is in the star - ry beam That falls a - long the Sum - mer sea.
bless the hour when first we met,— The hour that gave me love and thee!
colla voce.

CHORUS.

AIR.
O, Gen - e - vieve, Sweet Gen - e - vieve, The days may come, the days may go, But
ALTO.
TENOR.
O, Gen - e - vieve, Sweet Gen - e - vieve, The days may come, the days may go, But
BASS.
Coda, ad lib:
still the hands of mem-'ry weave The bliss - ful dreams of long a - go. O, Gen - e-vieve!
still the hands of mem-'ry weave The bliss - ful dreams of long a - go. O, Gen - e-vieve!
Coda, ad lib:
colla voce.

Tenting on the Old Camp Ground
WORDS & MUSIC BY
WALTER KITTREDGE,
Adapted & sung by the
HUTCHINSON FAMILY.
"TRIBE OF ASA"
3
BOSTON.
Published by Oliver Ditson & Co 277 Washington St.
Cinn. J.Church Jr.
N.York. W.A.Pond & Co.
Boston. J.C.Haynes & Co.
Phil.a J.E. Gould.
Entered according to act of Congress AD 1864 by O. Ditson & Co. in the Clerk's office of the Dist Court of Mass.

TENTING ON THE OLD CAMP GROUND.

Arranged by M.F.H. SMITH.

1 We're tent - ing to-night on the old Camp ground. Give us a song to cheer Our
2 We've been tent - ing to - night on the old Camp ground, Thinking of days gone by, Of the
3 We are tired of war on the old Camp ground, Many are dead and gone, Of the
4 We've been fight - ing to - day on the old Camp ground, Many are ly - ing near;
weary hearts, a song of home, And friends we love so dear.
lov'd ones at home that gave us the hand, And the tear that said, "Good bye!
brave and true who've left their homes, Others been wounded long.
Some are dead and some are dying, Many are in tears.
CHORUS.
Many are the hearts that are weary to-night, Wishing for the war to

cease;
Many are the hearts looking for the right To see the dawn of
peace.
Tenting to-night, Tenting to-night, Tenting on the old Camp
Last verse. Dying to-night, Dying to-night, (Omit.)
ground.
Last Time ppp.
Dying on the old Camp ground.
pp
ppp

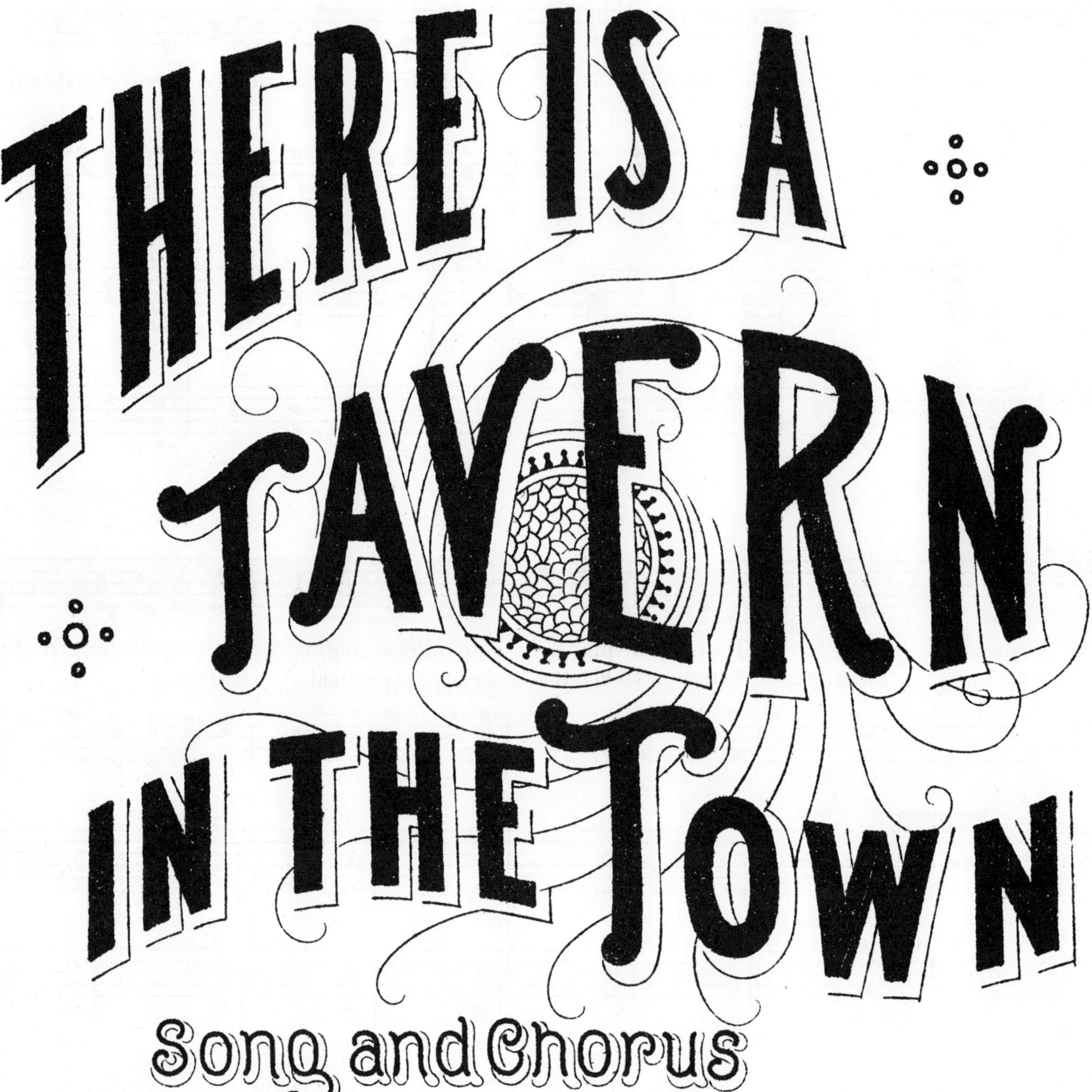

THE SEASONS SUCCESS.

Thorburn.

4

NEW YORK:
Willis Woodward & Co..
842 & 844 BROADWAY.

THERE IS A TAVERN IN THE TOWN.

Words and Music by F. J. ADAMS.

Andante. *cresc.*

mp *f* *p*

1. There is a tav-ern in the
2. He left me for a dam-sel
3. Oh! dig my grave both wide and

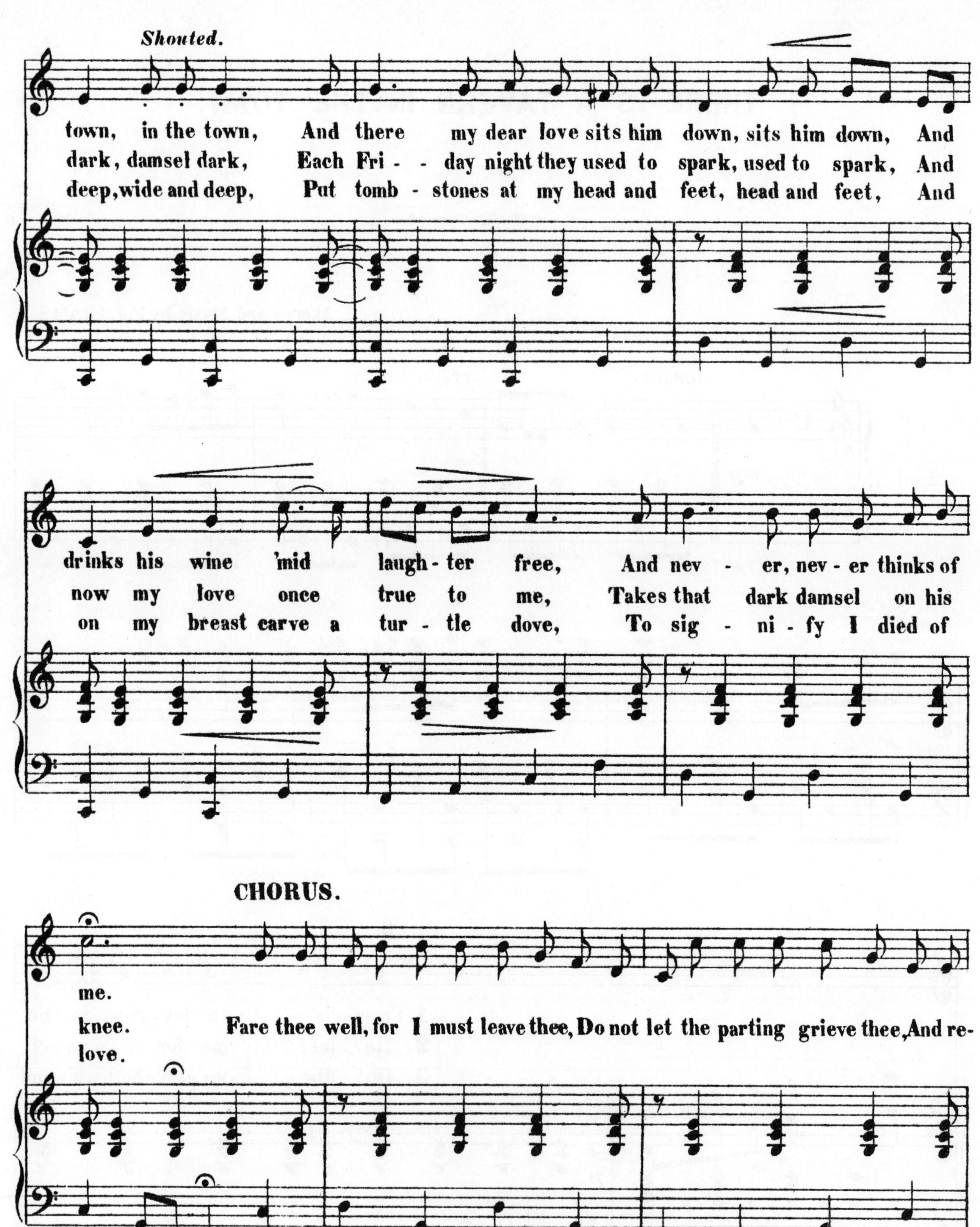
Shouted.
town, in the town, And there my dear love sits him down, sits him down, And
dark, damsel dark, Each Fri - - day night they used to spark, used to spark, And
deep, wide and deep, Put tomb - stones at my head and feet, head and feet, And
drinks his wine 'mid laugh - ter free, And nev - er, nev - er thinks of
now my love once true to me, Takes that dark damsel on his
on my breast carve a tur - tle dove, To sig - ni - fy I died of
CHORUS.
me.
knee. Fare thee well, for I must leave thee, Do not let the parting grieve thee, And re-
love.

-mem - ber that the best of friends must part, must part. A-
dieu, a - dieu, kind friends a - dieu, a - dieu, a - dieu, I can no lon - ger stay with
poco rit.
you, stay with you, I'll hang my harp on a weeping wil - low tree, And
poco rit.
1st. and 2d.
last time.
may the world go well with thee. thee.

THE VACANT CHAIR.
WITHIN SOUND OF THE ENEMY'S GUNS.
SILENT LUTE.
TRAMP! TRAMP! TRAMP!
or the
PRISONER'S HOPE.
AS SUNG BY EDWIN KELLEY,
OF ARLINGTON KELLEY & LEON'S MINSTRELS.
Song & Chorus.
BY GEO. F. ROOT.
BATTLE CRY OF FREEDOM
WHO'LL SAVE THE LEFT
Published by Root & Cady.
67 Washington St.
CHICAGO.
3
COPCUTT-WILLIAMS

TRAMP! TRAMP! TRAMP!

(THE PRISONER'S HOPE.)

all that I can do, Tho' I try to cheer my com - rades and be gay.
beat - en back dismayed, And we heard the cry of vict - 'ry o'er and o'er.
poor heart al - most gay, As we think of see - ing home and friends once more.

When the Chorus is sung, this may be omitted after the first verse.

Tramp, tramp, tramp, the boys are march - ing, Cheer up comrades they will come, And be-
Tramp, tramp, tramp, the boys are march - ing, Cheer up comrades they will come, And be-
Tramp, tramp, tramp, the boys are march - ing, Cheer up comrades they will come, And be-

CHORUS.
Air
Tramp, tramp, tramp, the boys are march - ing, Cheer up comrades they will come. And be-
Alto
Tramp, tramp, tramp, the boys are march-ing on, O cheer up com - rades they will come, And be-
Tenor
Tramp, tramp, tramp, the boys are march-ing, on, O cheer up com - rades . they will come, And be-
neath the star - ry flag We shall breathe the air a - gain, Of the free-land in our own be-lov-ed home.
neath the star - ry flag We shall breathe the air a - gain, Of the free-land in our own be-lov-ed home.
neath the star - ry flag We shall breathe the air a - gain, Of the free-land in our own be-lov-ed home.

Pr. 25 Cts. Net.

BALTIMORE,

Published by F. D. Benteen 131 Baltimore St.

"VIVE LA COMPAGNIE."

CHORUS.
Vi-ve la vi-ve la vi-ve l'amour, vi-ve la vi-ve la vi-ve l'amour.
Vi-ve la vi-ve la vi-ve l'amour, vi-ve la vi-ve la vi-ve l'amour.
Vi-ve la vi-ve la vi-ve l'amour, vi-ve la vi-ve la vi-ve l'amour.
Ped. Ped. Ped. Ped.
Vi-ve l'amour, vi-ve l'amour, vi-ve la com--pag--nie.
Vi-ve l'amour, vi-ve l'amour, vi-ve la com--pag--nie.
Vi-ve l'amour, vi-ve l'amour, vi-ve la com--pag--nie.
ff

SECOND VERSE.

3.

Let ev'ry married man— drink to his wife,
Vive la compagnie.
The friend of his bosom and comfort of life,
Vive la compagnie.
Oh! vive la &c.

4.

Come fill up your glasses— I'll give you a toast,
Vive la compagnie.
Here's a health to our friend— our kind, worthy host,
Vive la compagnie.
Oh! vive la &c.

5.

Since all, with good humor, I've toasted so free,
Vive la compagnie.
I hope it will please you to drink now with me,
Vive la compagnie.
Oh! vive la &c.

L. W. Webb.

Ethiopian Song

FOR THE

PIANO FORTE

BY

GEO. P. KNAUFF.

25 cts. net.

Published by F. D. BENTEEN *Baltimore*

W. T. MAYO *New Orleans*

WAIT FOR THE WAGON.

G. P. KNAUFF.

ev--'ry Sunday morning when I am by your side, We'll jump in--to the
Wagon, and all take a ride. Wait for the Wa-gon,
Wait for the Wa-gon, Wait for the Wagon and we'll all take a ride.
CHORUS.
Air.
Wait for the Wa-gon, Wait for the Wa-gon, Wait for the
Alto.
Tenor.
Wait for the Wa-gon, Wait for the Wa-gon, Wait for the
Bass.

2.

Where the river runs like silver, and the birds they sing so sweet,
I have a cabin, Phillis, and something good to eat.
Come listen to my story, it will relieve my heart,
So jump into the Wagon, and off we will start.
Wait for the Wagon &c.

3.

Do you believe my Phillis, dear, old Mike with all his wealth,
Can make you half so happy, as I with youth and health?
We'll have a little farm, a horse, a pig and cow;
And you will mind the dairy, while I will guide the plough.
Wait for the Wagon &c.

4.

Your lips are red as poppies, your hair so slick and neat,
All braided up with dahlias, and hollyhocks so sweet.
It's ev'ry Sunday morning, when I am by your side,
We'll jump into the Wagon, and all take a ride.
Wait for the Wagon &c.

5.

Together on life's journey, we'll travel till we stop,
And if we have no trouble, we'll reach the happy top.
Then come with me sweet Phillis, my dear, my lovely bride,
We'll jump into the Wagon, and all take a ride.
Wait for the Wagon &c.

Webb.

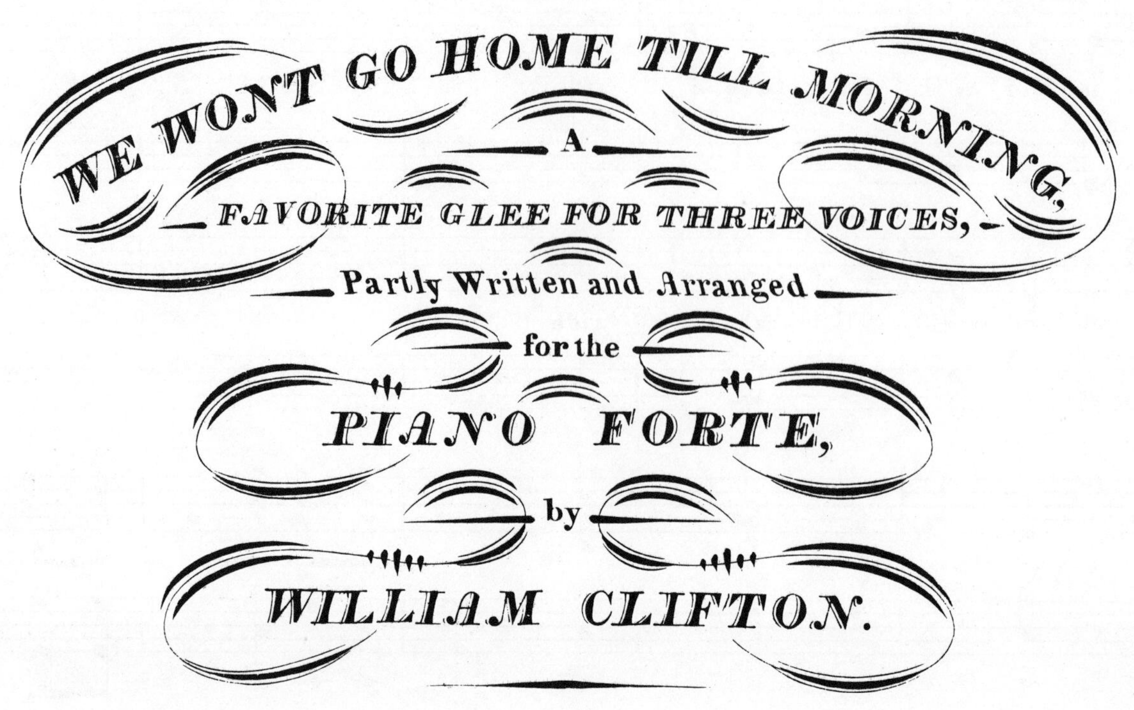

BOSTON Published by OLIVER DITSON 115 Washington St.

Air.
We're all met here to_geth_ _er, We're all met here to_geth_ _er, We're
Tenor.
We're all met here to_geth_ _er, We're all met here to_geth_ _er, We're
Bass.
We're all met here to_geth_ _er, We're all met here to_geth_ _er, We're
p
Coda
all met here to_geth_ _er. To eat and drink good cheer; To
all met here to_geth_ _er, To eat and drink good cheer; To
all met here to_geth_ _er, To eat and drink good cheer;
f
A_ _way a_way a_ _ _ _way A_ _way a_way a_ _ _ _way, For
eat and drink good cheer, To eat and drink good cheer, For we
eat and drink good cheer, To eat and drink good cheer, For we
For we
p

2

We'll sing, we'll dance and be merry,
We'll sing, we'll dance and be merry,
We'll sing, we'll dance and be merry,
And kiss the lasses dear;
And kiss the lasses dear;
And kiss the lasses dear;
For we wont go home &c.

3

The girls we love them dearly,
The girls we love them dearly,
The girls we love them dearly,
And they love us, tis clear;
And they love us, tis clear;
And they love us, tis clear;
So we wont go home &c.

After singing the last Verse, finish with the Coda, Away away &c.

To his friend
Edwin Green, Esq.

When I saw sweet Nellie home

Ballad

SUNG BY

MR. D. S. WAMBOLD.

Composed and arranged by

JOHN FLETCHER.

An unauthorized and incorrect copy of this song has been published under my name but without my consent This is the ONLY CORRECT EDITION

J. Fletcher

Published by Wm. A. POND & Co. 347 Broadway

Boston O. DITSON & CO.

Pittsburgh. H. KLEBER & BRO.

Cincinnati. C. Y. FONDA.

3

WHEN I SAW SWEET NELLY HOME.

JOHN FLETCHER.

fell Hush'd the sound of day_light bustle Closed the pink_eyed pim_per
gold In the lawn by el_ders shaded I my love to Nel_ly
brow But a love smile cheers and blesses Life's de_clin_ing mo_ments
nell As a_down the moss grown wood path Where the cattle love to
told As we stood to_geth_er gaz_ing On the star be_spangled
now Ma_tron in the snow_y ker_chief Clo_ser to my bo_som
roam From an au_gust evening par_ty I was see_ing Nelly home
dome How I blessed the au_gust evening When I saw sweet Nelly home
come Tell me do'st thou still re_mem_ber When I saw sweet Nelly home
ritard

Repeat Chorus last time PP
TENOR
In the sky the bright stars glittered On the grass the moonlight
ALTO
AIR
In the sky the bright stars glittered On the grass the moonlight
BASS
shone From an august eve_ning party I was see_ing Nelly home.
shone From an august eve_ning party I was see_ing Nelly home.
last time

To the

Army & Navy

OF THE UINON.

When Johnny comes marching home

Music introduced in the Soldier's Return March.

BY

GILMORE'S BAND

WORDS & MUSIC BY

LOUIS LAMBERT.

3

BOSTON.

Published by Henry Tolman & Co. 291 Washington St.

WHEN JOHNNY COMES MARCHING HOME.

Chorus. Repeat ad lib.
all turn out, And we'll all feel gay, When Johnny comes marching home.
strew the way, And we'll all feel gay, When Johnny comes marching home.
f
fp
fp
ff
Solo.
Chorus.
3. Get rea - dy for the Ju - bi - lee, Hur - rah, Hur -
4. Let love and friendship on that day, Hur - rah, Hur -
ff
Solo.
Chorus.
- rah, We'll give the he - ro three times three, Hurrah, Hur - rah, The
- rah, Their choic - est treasures then display, Hurrah, Hur - rah, And
p
ff

Chorus.
laur-el wreath is rea-dy now, To place up-on his loyal brow, And we'll
let each one perform some part, To fill with joy the warriors heart, And we'll
p
all feel gay, When Johnny comes marching home.
all feel gay, When Johnny comes marching home.
f
fp
fp
f

Inscribed to Mrs. S. L. Atwell.

When You and I were Young, Maggie;

SONG AND CHORUS.

WORDS BY

GEORGE W. JOHNSON,

MUSIC BY

J. A. BUTTERFIELD.

GUITAR 2½ PIANO 3.

CHICAGO:
PUBLISHED BY J A BUTTERFIELD, 37 CROSBY OPERA HOUSE

When you and I were Young.

Words by GEO. W. JOHNSON.

Music by J. A. BUTTERFIELD.

we used to long a - - - go. The green grove is gone from the
each found a place of rest, Is built where the birds used to
time a - - lone was the pen. They say we are a - ged and
hill, Mag-gie, Where first the dai - sies sprung; The
play, Mag-gie, And join in the songs that were sung: For we
gray, Mag-gie, As sprays by the white breakers flung; But to
creak - ing old mill is still, Maggie, Since you and I were young.
sang as gay as they, Maggie, When you and I were young.
me you're as fair as you were, Maggie, When you and I were young.

CHORUS.

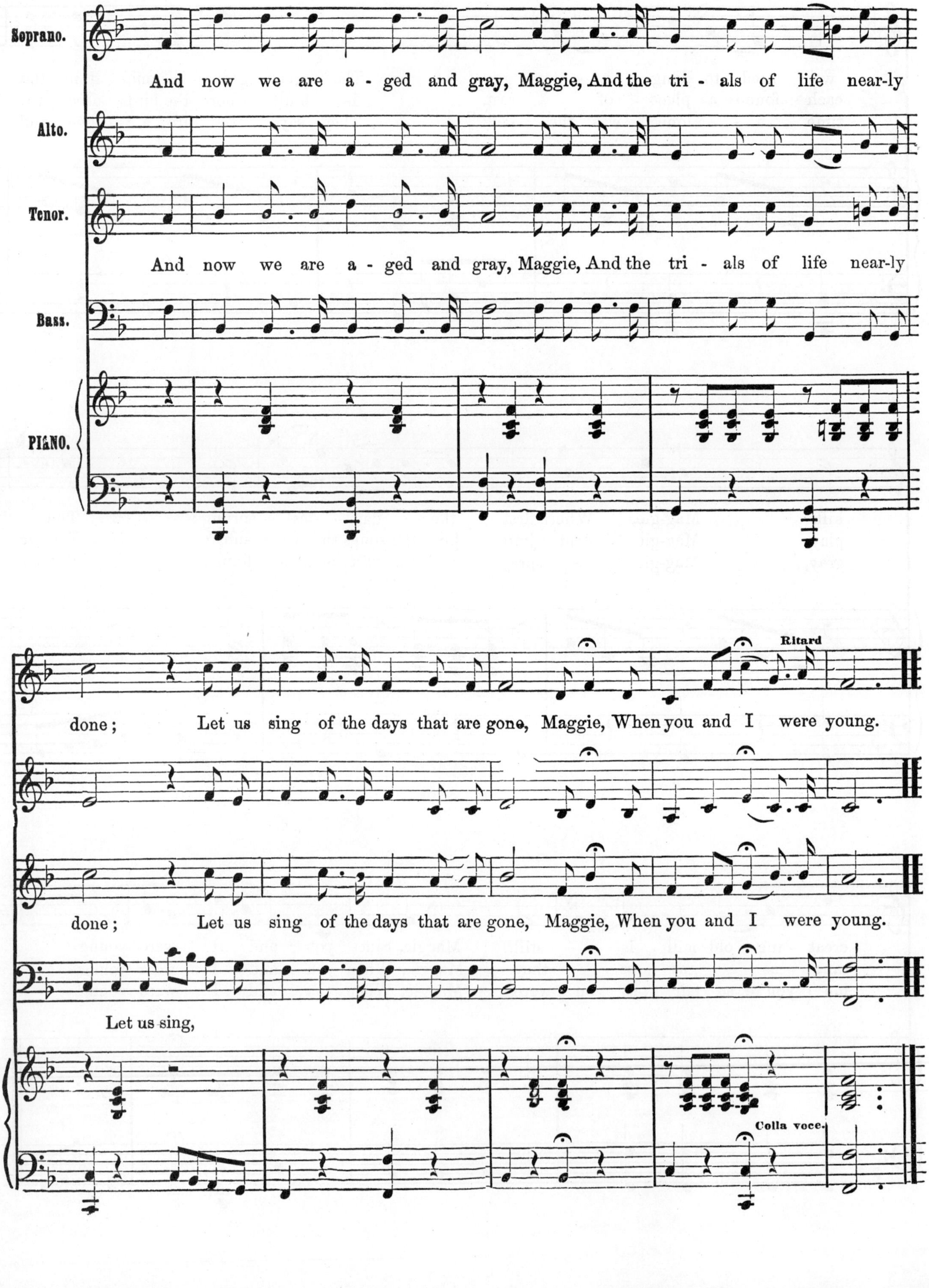

Soprano.

And now we are a - ged and gray, Maggie, And the tri - als of life near-ly

Alto.

Tenor.

And now we are a - ged and gray, Maggie, And the tri - als of life near-ly

Bass.

PIANO.

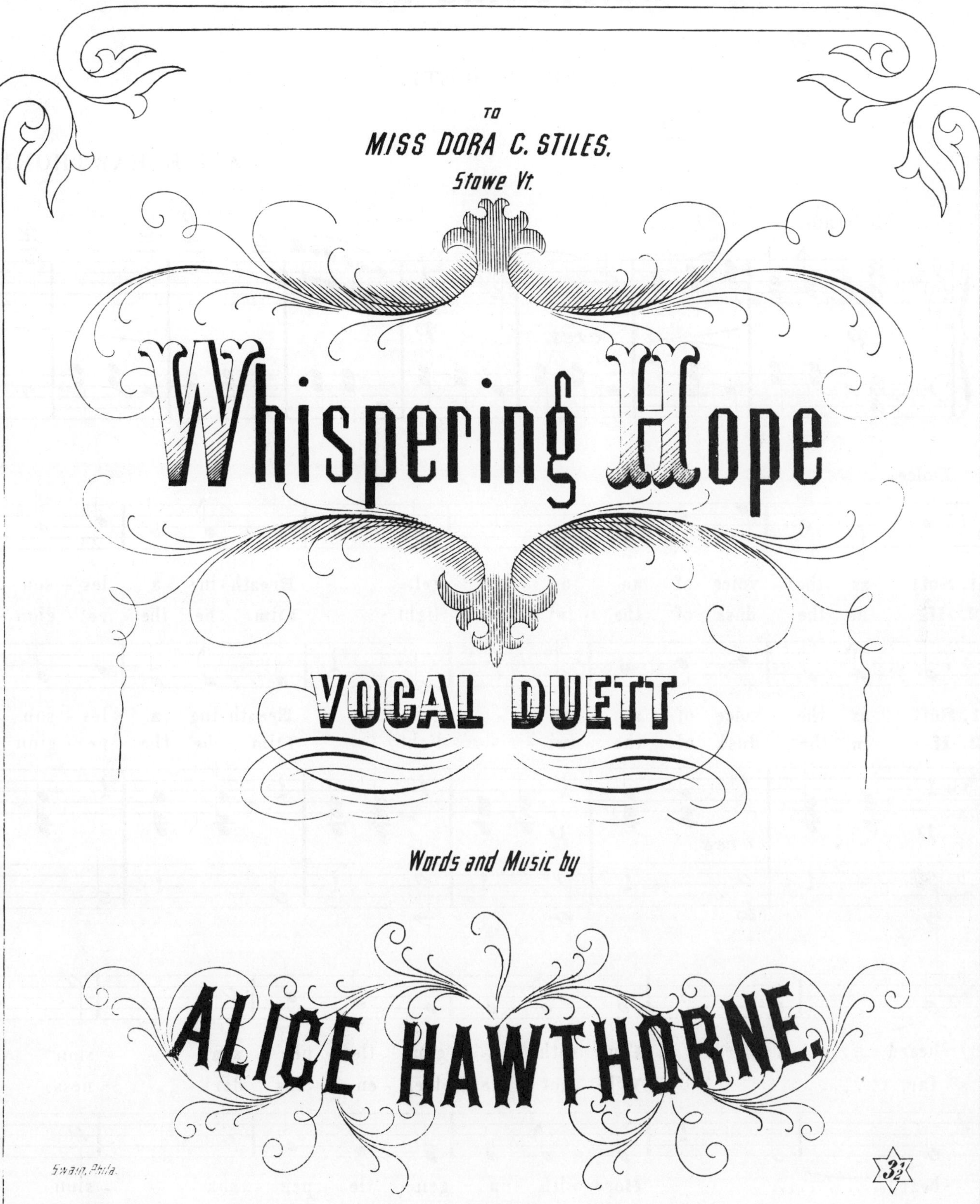

PHILADELPHIA

PUBLISHED BY LEE & WALKER 922 CHESTNUT ST.

W. H. Boner & Co. 1102 Chestnut St.

Chas. W. Harris, N. York.

WHISPERING HOPE

VOCAL DUETT.

ALICE HAWTHORNE.

Whis - pers her com-fort - ing word.............
Bright - en the glim - mer - ing star?...........
Wait, till the dark - ness is
Then when the night is up-
Whis - pers her com-fort - ing word.............
Bright - en the glim - mer - ing star?...........
Wait, till the dark - ness is
Then when the night is up-
o - - - - ver
-on us
Wait, till the tem - pest is done...........
Why should the heart sink a - way...........
rit.
o - - - - ver
-on us
Wait, till the tem - pest is done...........
Why should the heart sink a - way...........
rit.
rit.
tempo.
Hope for the sun - shine to - mor - - - row,
When the dark mid - night is o - - - - ver
Af - ter the show - er is
Watch for the break - ing of
Hope for the sun - shine to - mor - - - row,
When the dark mid - night is o - - - - ver
Af - ter the show - er is
Watch for the break - ing of
tempo.

gone . . . .
day . . . .
Whis - - - - - - per - ing
Hope . . . .
Oh how
gone . . . .
day . . . .
Whis - per - ing
Hope
Whis-per-ing
Hope
well - - - - - - - - come thy
voice . . . .
Mak - - - - - - - - - - ing my
Wel - come thy
voice
Oh
how
wel - come thy
voice
Mak
ing my
heart
heart . . . .
in
its
sor - - - - - - - row
re - - joice . . . .
Mak - ing my
heart in
its
sor - - - - row
re - - joice . . . .

Whis - - - - - - - per - ing Hope . . . . Oh how wel - - - - - - - come thy
Whis - per - ing Hope Whis - per - ing Hope Wel - come thy voice oh how
voice . . . . Mak - - - - - - - ing my heart . . . . in its
Wel - come thy voice Mak - ing my heart Mak - ing my heart in its
sor - - - - - - - - row re - - joice . . . .
sor - - - - - - row re - - joice . . . .

WOODMAN! SPARE THAT TREE!

A BALLAD

Lithoᵈ. of Endicott N.Y.

THE WORDS COPIED FROM THE NEW YORK MIRROR, WRITTEN BY

GEORGE P. MORRIS,

BY WHOM THIS SONG IS RESPECTFULLY DEDICATED TO

BENJAMIN M. BROWN, ESQ.

THE MUSIC BY

Henry Russel.

New York, Published by FIRTH & HALL, No. 1, Franklin-Sq.

In presenting the song of "Woodman! spare that tree!" to the public, the Publishers, at the suggestion of Mr. Russell, take the liberty of accompanying it with the following graphic and touching letter, which, although written exclusively for private perusal, will deeply interest those who have read the admirable ballad whose simplicity, terseness and pathos, it so exquisitely conveys in the melody of sound.

New-York Mirror Office,
February 1, 1837.

My dear sir,—You did me the honour to request some lines of mine for music; and, at the moment, being delighted with your fine voice and exquisite taste in singing, I said I would write you a song. Now, I think with our friend Knowles, that a promise given, when it can be kept, admits not of release, "save by consent or forfeiture of those who hold it," and so I have been as good as my word, as you will perceive by the enclosure of "The Oak." I hope it will answer your purpose. Let me tell you how I came to choose an old tree for my subject. Riding out of town on horseback, a few days since, in company with a friend, who was once the expectant heir of the largest estate in America, but over whose worldly prospects a blight has recently come, he invited me to turn down a little romantick woodland pass not far from Bloomingdale. "Your object?" inquired I. "Merely to look once more at an old tree planted by my grandfather, near a cottage that was once my father's." "The place is your's then?" said I. "No, my poor mother sold it;" and I observed a slight quiver of the lip, at the recollection of that circumstance. "Dear mother!" resumed my companion, "we passed many happy, *happy* days, in that old cottage; but it's nothing to me now—father, mother, sisters, cottage—all, all, gone;" and a paleness over-spread his fine countenance, and a moisture came to his eyes as he spoke. But after a moment's pause, he said, "Don't think me foolish: I don't know how it is, I never ride out but I turn down this lane to look at that old tree. I have a thousand recollections about it, and I always greet it as a familiar and well-remembered friend. In the by-gone summer-time it was a friend indeed. I often listened to the good counsel of my parents there, and I have had *such* gambols with my sisters! Its leaves are all off now, so you won't see it to half its advantage, for it is a glorious old fellow in summer; but *I* like it full as well in very winter time." These words were scarcely uttered, when my companion cried out, "There it is!" and he sprang from his saddle and ran toward it. I soon overtook him, wondering at his haste; but what met my sight, made it no wonder. Near the tree stood an old man with his coat off, sharpening an axe. He was the occupant of the cottage. "What are you going to do with that axe?" "What's that to you," was the reply. "A little matter, but not much—you're not going to cut it down surely?" "Yes, but I am though," said the woodman. "What for," inquired my companion, almost choaked with emotion. "What for? why, because I think proper to do so: what for? I like that! Well, I'll tell you what for: this tree makes my dwelling unhealthy: it stands too near the house; prevents the moisture from exhaling, and renders us all liable to fever-and-ague." "Who told you that?" "Why, Dr. ——." "Have you any other reason for wishing to cut it down?" "Yes, I am getting old, the woods are a great way off, and this tree is of some value to me to burn." He was soon convinced, however, that the story about the fever-and-ague was a mere fiction, for there never had been a case of that disease in its neighbourhood; and then was asked what the tree was worth for firewood? "Why, when it is down about ten dollars." "Suppose I should give you that sum, would you let it stand?" "Yes." "You're sure of that?" "Positive." "Then draw me a bond to that effect." I drew it up; it was witnessed by his daughter; the money was paid, and we left the place, with an assurance from the young girl, who looked as smiling and beautiful as a Hebe, that the tree should stand as long as she lived. We returned to the turnpike, and pursued our ride. These circumstances made a strong impression upon my mind, and furnished me with the materials for the song I send you. I hope you will like it, and pardon me for this long and hurried letter.

With sentiments of respect,
I remain,
Yours, very truly,
GEO. P. MORRIS.

Henry Russell, Esq

WOODMAN SPARE THAT TREE.

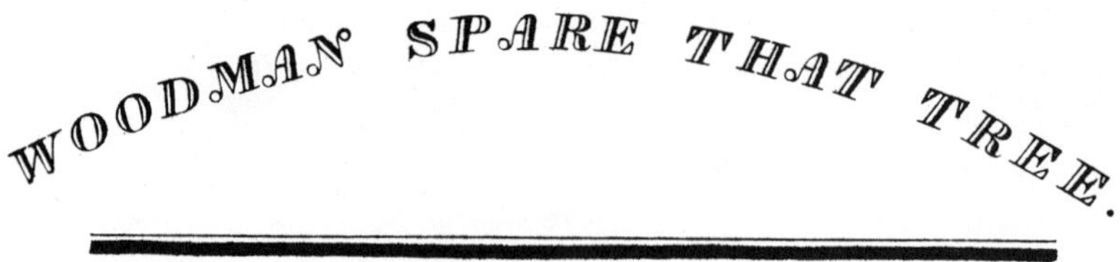

Pr: 50.

Words by George P. Morris. Esq.r

Music by Henry Russell.

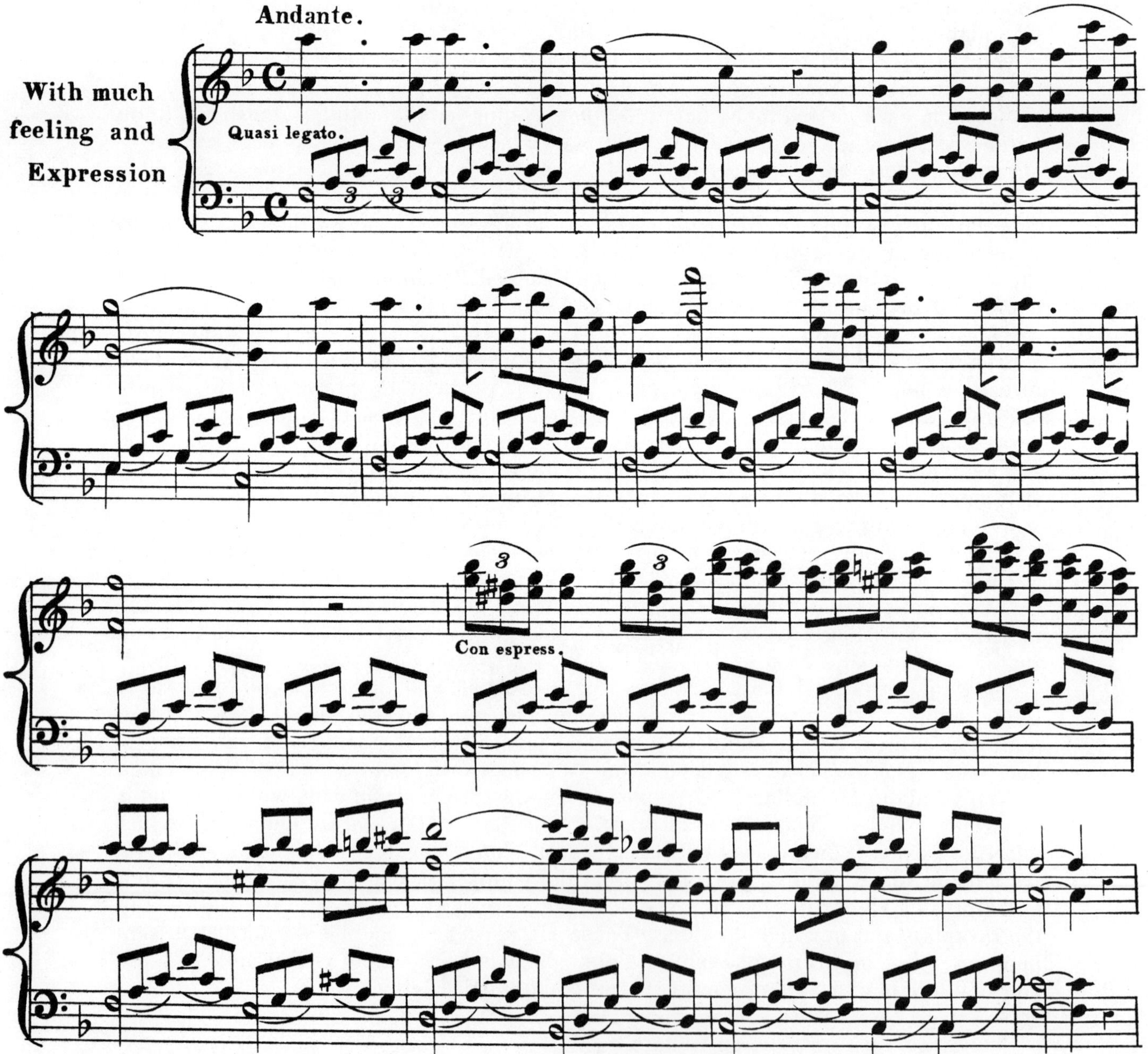

With much feeling and Expression
Andante.
Quasi legato.
Con espress.

 3

Wood----man spare that tree! Touch not a sin--- gle
bough; In youth it shelterd me, And
I'll protect it now; 'Twas my fore fa---ther's
hand That placed it near his cot, There,

wood - - - - man, let it stand, Thy axe shall harm it
not!

That old fami - - - liar tree, Whose glo - - - ry and re - - - -
nown Are spread o'er land and sea, And
Con anima.
wouldst thou hack it down?
Wood-man, for-bear thy-
stroke! Cut not its earth, bound ties; Oh!

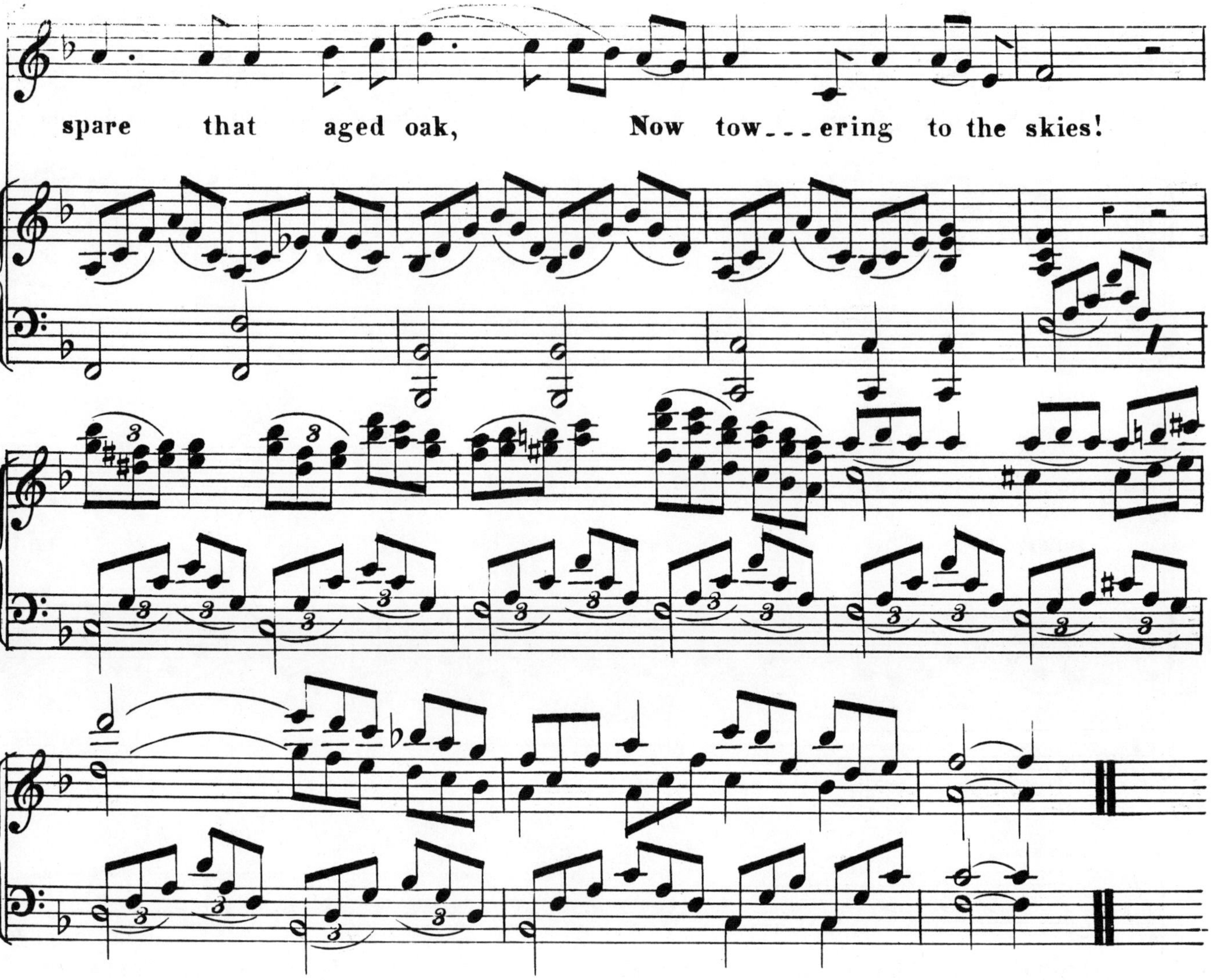

spare that aged oak, Now tow- - - ering to the skies!

3

When but an idle boy
  I sought its grateful shade;
In all their gushing joy
  Here, too, my sisters played.
My mother kiss'd me here;
  My father press'd my hand –
Forgive this foolish tear,
  But let that old oak stand!

4

My heart-strings round thee cling,
  Close as thy bark, old friend!
Here shall the wild-bird sing,
  And still thy branches bend.
Old tree! the storm still brave!
  And, woodman, leave the spot;
While I've a hand to save,
  Thy axe shall harm it not.

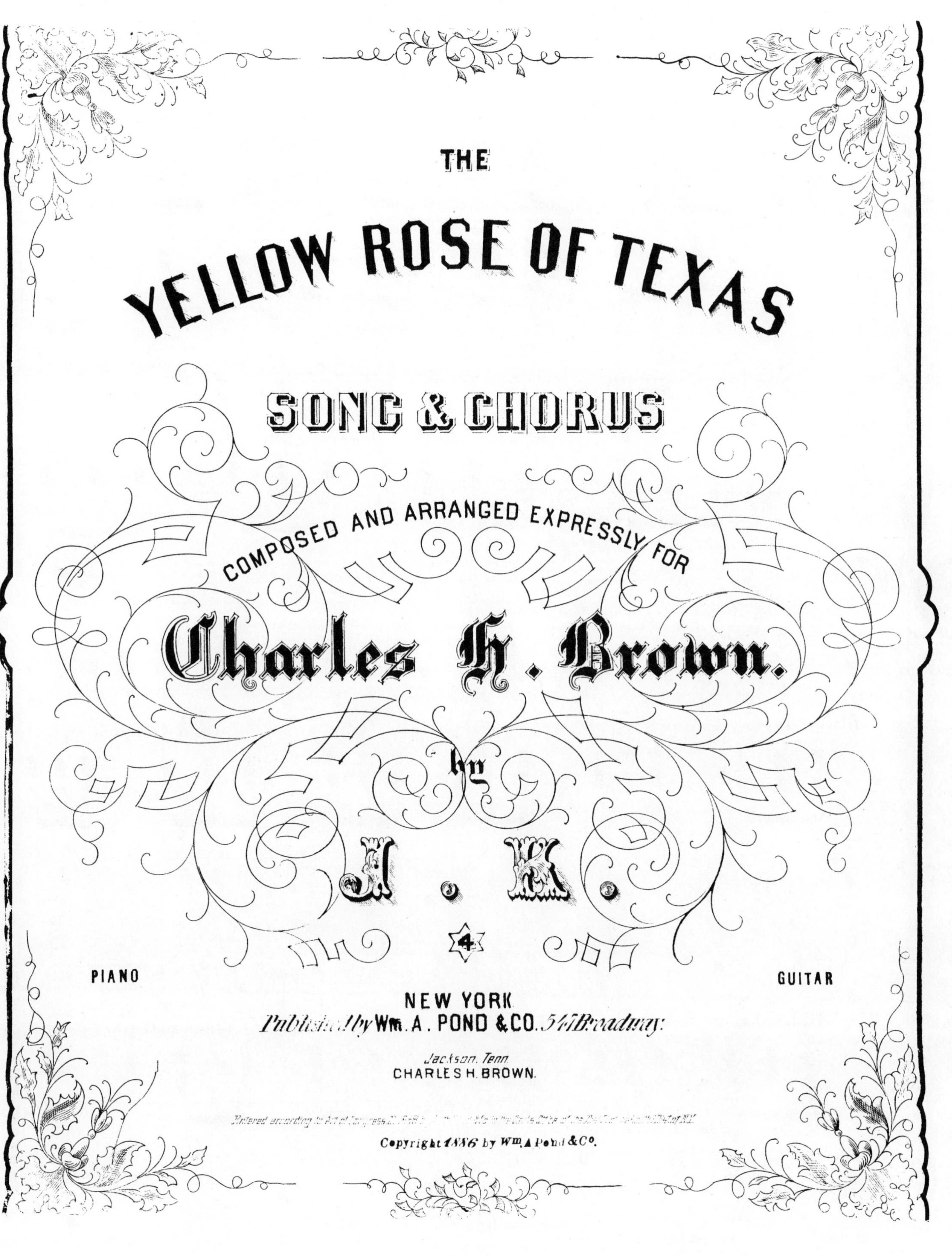
THE
YELLOW ROSE OF TEXAS
SONG & CHORUS
COMPOSED AND ARRANGED EXPRESSLY FOR
Charles H. Brown.
by
J. K.
4
PIANO
GUITAR
NEW YORK
Published by Wm. A. POND & CO. 547 Broadway.
Jackson, Tenn.
CHARLES H. BROWN.
Copyright 1886 by Wm. A. Pond & Co.

THE YELLOW ROSE OF TEXAS
ALLEGRETTO.
There's a yel_low rose in Texas that I am going to see, No
other darkey knows her, no darkey only me; She cried so when I left her, it
like to broke my heart, And if I e_ver find her we never more will part.

CHORUS.
She's the sweetest rose of color this darkey ever knew, Her
She's the sweetest rose of color this darkey ever knew, Her
p
Staccato.
eyes are bright as diamonds, they sparkle like the dew, You may talk about your Dearest May, and
eyes are bright as diamonds, they sparkle like the dew, You may talk about your Dearest May, and

sing of Rosa Lee, But the yellow rose of Texas beats the belles of Tennessee.
sing of Rosa Lee, But the yellow rose of Texas beats the belles of Tennessee.

2d. VERSE.
Where the Ri_o Grande is flowing, and the starry skies are bright, She
walks a_long the ri_ver in the quiet sum_mer night; She
thinks if I re_member, when we parted long a_go, I
promis'd to come back again, and not to leave her so. (CHORUS) She's the sweetest &c.
3d. VERSE.
Oh! now I'm going to find her, for my heart is full of woe, And we'll
sing the song to_gether, that we sung so long a_go; We'll
play the ban_jo gaily, and we'll sing the songs of yore, And the
yellow rose of Texas shall be mine for ever_more. (CHORUS)

Quidor, Engr.

ZIP COON,

A favorite Comic Song,

Litho: of Endicott, 359, Broadway

Sung by

MR. G. W. DIXON.

New York, Published by J. L. HEWITT & Co. *137, Broadway*

ZIP COON.

PIANO
FORTE.
ALLEGRO MAESTOSO.
O ole Zip Coon he is a larned skoler, O
ole Zip Coon he is a larned skolar, O ole Zip Coon he is a larned skolar, Sings
posum up a gum tree an coony in a holler. posum up a gum tree, coony on a stump,
posum up a gum tree, coony on a stump, posum up a gum tree coony on a stump, Den

2

O its old Suky blue skin, she is in lub wid me
I went the udder arter noon to take a dish ob tea;
What do you tink now, Suky hab for supper,
Why chicken foot an posum heel, widout any butter.

3

Did you eber see the wild goose, sailing on de occean,
O de wild goose motion is a bery pretty notion;
Ebry time de wild goose, beckens to de swaller,
You hear him google google google google gollar.

4

I went down to Sandy Hollar t other arternoon
And the first man I chanced to meet war ole Zip Coon;
Ole Zip Coon he is a natty scholar,
For he plays upon de Banjo "Cooney in de hollar."

5

My old Missus she's mad wid me,
Kase I would'nt go wid her into Tennessee
Massa build him barn and put in de fodder
Twas dis ting and dat ting one ting or odder.

6

I pose you heard ob de battle New Orleans,
Whar ole Gineral Jackson gib de British beans;
Dare de Yankee boys do de job so slick,
For dey cotch old Packenham an rowed him up de creek.

7

I hab many tings to tork about, but dont know wich come first,
So here de toast to old Zip Coon before he gin to rust;
May he hab de pretty girls, like de King ob ole,
To sing dis song so many times, 'fore he turn to mole.

Notes on the Music

Adeste Fideles

This favorite Christmas hymn is believed to date from 1740–43 and is attributed to John Francis Wade (ca. 1710–1786), an English music copyist and teacher. It is not really known why the piece came to be called the "Portuguese Hymn," though Wade did make a manuscript copy for the English College in Lisbon. The Latin words with the music were published together for the first time in *An Essay on the Church Plain Chant* (London, 1782), but the standard English translation by Frederick Oakeley did not appear until 1841. The text was revised with the familiar opening line "O come, all ye faithful" by James R. Murray, and in this form first appeared in 1852.

The edition reprinted here, under the title "Adeste Fideles, The favorite Portuguez [*sic*] hymn On the Nativity," was published around 1803 by John and Michael Paff at their music shop in Maiden Lane in New York. It is among the earliest printings of the hymn in the United States (the first here was in Benjamin Carr's *Musical Journal*, Vol. II, 1800). In the Paff edition the verse section is set for a solo voice (or chorus in unison) with the refrain marked "Duo" at the repetition of "venite adoremus" and "Coro" at the last phrase, which is written out in open score on four staves. (There is a separate keyboard accompaniment throughout the piece.) This canonic treatment of the voices in the refrain is a key feature of the fuguing tunes so popular in the late eighteenth and early nineteenth centuries in England and America, with William Billings one of the prominent practitioners of the form. The only differences between this early edition and that of the modern hymnal lie in rhythmic variations here and there and in the time signature. Most earlier versions are in 2/4, whereas current versions even out the meter into 4/4 for modern congregations. This is unfortunate, for the briskness and swing suggested by the 2/4 meter seems more appropriate to the rather ecstatic nature of the piece with its repetitions and cumulative power.

All Quiet Along the Potomac To-Night

This widely popular Civil War poem, which was set by both Northern and Southern composers, was first published in *Harper's Weekly* (November 30, 1861) under the title "A Picket Shot." The poem was signed with the initials E. L. B., referring to Mrs. Ethel Lynn Beers of Goshen, New York. There have been various claims of authorship for the poem, especially by the Mississippian Lamar Fontaine (his case is presented in Johnson's *Our Familiar Songs and Those Who Made Them*, page 563), but Mrs. Beers is now firmly established as the author. The phrase "All quiet along the Potomac," however, did not originate with her. Irvin Silber, an authority on Civil War songs, and others have pointed out that the phrase was commonly used in newspapers at the beginning of the war. This is undoubtedly what led the author to set off the phrase in quotation marks. Despite the fact that the poem deals with a theme well-worked in popular literature of the day—the death of a lonely soldier far from home—it is unusually strong and direct.

The musical setting by John Hill Hewitt—the best known of the various settings and popular in both the South and North—adds a comment of its own. The bright, almost frivolous tune with its waltzing 6/8 accompaniment creates a double irony as vehicle for the grim business of the text.

Hewitt (1801–1890) was the son of the English immigrant James Hewitt, who became so important in the musical life of New York and Boston as composer and publisher after his arrival in 1792. John Hewitt was educated at West Point and was widely read in law and literature. He was a resident of Baltimore for many years, becoming a rather formidable figure as poet (he was known as the Bard of the Confederacy), journalist, editor and composer (he wrote dozens of songs and several stage works). He loved music but became disillusioned with the musical career. He summed up his feelings on the subject in his charming memoir *Shadows on the Wall* (1877):

My ballads are (or *were*) well known throughout the country; for I have not published for many years. Why? the reader may ask. For the simple reason that it does not pay the author; the publisher pockets all, and gets rich on the brains of the poor fool who is chasing that *ignis fatuus*, reputation.

America (My Country! 'Tis of Thee)

The text of this patriotic hymn, which is perhaps second only to "The Star Spangled Banner" as the most venerable national song, was written in 1831 by Samuel Francis Smith (1808–1895), Harvard graduate, clergyman and professor of modern languages. The tune, of course, originated with "God Save the King," the English national anthem first published in 1744. The music is of unknown authorship although there have been many claimants, Henry Carey perhaps chief among them. The tune was published in the American colonies in the eighteenth century (e.g., in James Lyon's hymn collection *Urania*, 1761) and was used with various texts. Smith's verses (originally five) were written for Lowell Mason (1792–1872), the pioneer in popular music education, editor and composer of about twelve hundred hymns. Mason was at the time organist at the Park Street Church in Boston, and it was here that "America" was performed for the first time at a children's celebration on the 4th of July, 1831, with Mason conducting. Shortly after, he gave the song its first publication in his hymn collection *The Choir* (Boston, 1832). It appeared subsequently in a sheet-music edition as "My Country! 'Tis of Thee," published by C. Bradlee of Boston.

The Arkansas Traveller

This is the only piece in the collection that is not a song: it is a dialogue—an antique American comedy routine, actually—with music. Traditionally the dialogue seems most often to have been delivered by a single performer and the tune played on a violin (to mirror the situation in the text). The music has been adapted for several song versions, each with a different set of verses, but this was not done until the twentieth century. The edition of "The Arkansas Traveller" reprinted here, published by Ditson probably in 1863, credits the piece to Mose Case, an itinerant black guitarist about whom little is apparently known. Actually it is Case's version of a piece that was known in oral tradition before 1850, and the music (without the dialogue) first appeared in print in 1847. Where and with whom the piece originated is not known. The music, which consists of only two strains of eight bars each, might be of folk origin; its style is similar to many anonymous fiddle tunes of the Southern mountains. An excellent résumé of the history of the piece and the various claims of authorship may be found in "Arkansas Traveler—A Multi-Parented Wayfarer," a 1971 article by Mary D. Hudgins (see Bibliography).

The title page of the Ditson edition features a variation of an American "primitive" illustration used in earlier editions of the piece, but it is by far the most individual treatment of the subject. The clever and carefully executed details—from the figure glimpsed through the door of the cabin to the marvelous rickrack fence and handsome border design—show the hand of a very talented craftsman. His name was H. F. Greene (the surname appears fairly often on Ditson covers of the 1850s and '60s) and he signed his picture in the lower left corner of the border.

Aura Lea

"Aura Lea" is one of that rather special group of antique American popular songs that transcended the particular purpose for which they were written and somehow survived in one form or another far beyond the life expectancy of products that by usual definition are ephemeral. It is as if they had been placed in a time machine that kept them ever fresh and useful. "Aura Lea" was published in 1861 in Cincinnati and it was intended for use on the minstrel stage; it is dedicated to S. C. Campbell of Hooley and Campbell's Minstrels, one of the traveling groups of the time. It became quite popular during the Civil War era, apparently in both the North and South: one source refers to its being sung by Northern troops, and it was published at least once in the Confederacy (Richmond, 1864).

The delicate poem—a little apostrophe to the "Maid of golden hair"—is by William Whiteman Fosdick (1825–1862), a Cincinnati writer who was considered significant enough for inclusion in the *Dictionary of American Biography*. Fosdick's contribution, however, did not prove indispensable to the life of the song; it also survives in two transformations with verses by one L. W. Becklaw, in one instance, and by Elvis Presley and Vera Matson in the second.

The Becklaw version was apparently fashioned in 1865 for the graduating class at West Point, perhaps as a result of the song's popularity with Union troops. This version is, of course, the well-known "Army Blue," beginning with the lines:

> We've not much longer here to stay,
> For in a month or two
> We'll bid farewell to "Cadet Gray,"
> And don the "Army Blue."

(Becklaw's text fits the tune well enough except at the word "Cadet," which suffers a misplaced accent.) Published collections of West Point songs identify "Army Blue" as the "Song of the Class of 1865," with "Aura Lea" occasionally credited as the source of the tune.

The Presley-Matson version was created in 1956 as the title song for Presley's movie debut in *Love Me Tender.* Since the movie's plot involves a family just after the Civil War, someone had the idea of using an authentic song from the period; with a little reworking and new lyrics, "Aura Lea" became "Love Me Tender" and served nicely. It also provided Presley with one of his best-selling recordings.

It is, of course, the music of "Aura Lea" that holds the key to its longevity. In the original edition, we see it in its pristine state: simple, memorable, carefully crafted, with touches of rhythmic and harmonic subtlety. Later versions are somewhat bland by comparison and lack the charm of the original.

The composer of this durable piece is George R. Poulton, who did not fare as well as the poet Fosdick in securing a place in the reference books. He did, however, find a place in the files of the Historical Society of Lansingburgh, New York, and Mr. Warren F. Broderick of the Society generously supplied information on the composer. Poulton was born in England in 1828 and at age seven was brought by his parents to Lansingburgh. While still in his teens he began organizing local concerts and gained a reputation as violinist, pianist, singer and conductor. In the late 1840s he also began to see his compositions published, and before his death at age 39 in Lansingburgh, at least 22 songs and piano pieces were issued by houses in New York City, Rochester, Buffalo and elsewhere. During his brief career as composer and music teacher in several towns in upper New York State, Poulton also gained a reputation of another kind—that of rake and hell-raiser—and he has the distinction of being one of what must surely be a very select group of American composers to be literally tarred and feathered. One looks at Poulton's portrait on the covers of his "Albion Polka" and "Willie Bell," with his slight smile and shoulder-length hair, and wonders what was on the mind of the composer of the demure "Aura Lea."

The Battle Cry of Freedom

George Frederick Root (1820–1895) was a leading figure in the establishment and spread of music education in the United States. He was already an eminent figure in this field, as well as a successful composer and editor of school music collections, when he moved to Chicago from Connecticut in 1860 to join the firm of Root & Cady. This important music house had been founded two years earlier by Ebenezer T. Root (George's younger brother) and Chauncey M. Cady. The financial success of the company was established with a series of amazingly popular Civil War songs (three of which are reproduced in this collection). Root's own "The Battle Cry of Freedom" (1862) was the company's first runaway best seller and one of the memorable rallying songs of the war.

Root's autobiography of 1891 contains his account of the song's creation—how he was stirred by Lincoln's second call for troops, how the words and music then came together in a matter of hours, how the song was performed immediately at a huge rally (on July 26, 1862) with the ink hardly dry on the manuscript—but the story cannot be taken wholly at face value. Dena Epstein relates in her splendid history of the Root & Cady firm (see Bibliography) that Root had a slip of memory here, that the song was actually composed and performed somewhat earlier than he had remembered. Looking at the famous song well over a century after its creation, one can preceive perhaps only dimly its original power. Apart from the strong infectious tune, the text seems now quite pallid, with the exception of one line: "And altho' he may be poor, he shall never be a slave." Maybe it was just this sentiment, as well as the good tune, that fired the interest of another composer of abolitionist leanings—Root's friend Louis Moreau Gottschalk—who borrowed the song and took it into the recital hall in his virtuoso piano transcription "Battle Cry of Freedom (or Le Cri de Délivrance), Grand Caprice de concert" (1863–64).

Battle Hymn of the Republic

One of the few indisputable facts about the still-clouded origins of this apparently indestructible song is that the five verses were written by Julia Ward Howe in November 1861 in Washington, D.C. Mrs. Howe (1819–1910), wife of Dr. Samuel G. Howe, was a prominent liberal reformer and propagandist, a poet, and for a time a Unitarian minister. The poem (without the "Glory Hallelujah" refrain—this was not written by Mrs. Howe) was published first in the *New-York Daily Tribune* (January 14, 1862) and *The Atlantic Monthly* (February 1862).

The melody of the song (and the "Glory Hallelujah" refrain) seems to have originated with the Methodist hymn "Say, Brothers, Will You Meet Us?" copyrighted in New York by G. S. Scofield in 1858, which appeared in a few hymn collections at the time. During 1861, the first year of the Civil War, the music was used with new topical texts by Northern troops in Massachusetts and New York and was published that year in various editions as "John Brown," "The Popular John Brown Song" and "Glory Hallelujah." It is these versions which begin with the line "John Brown's body lies a mouldering in the grave," referring to a Sergeant John Brown at Fort Warren in Massachusetts (not to the famous John Brown of the Harper's Ferry raid). None of these editions credited a specific composer or author.

As can be seen from the facsimile in this collection, the first edition of "Battle Hymn of the Republic" was published in 1862 by Oliver Ditson as a solo song with chorus in three parts (two trebles and a bass). The title page indicates that it is "Adapted to the favorite Melody of 'Glory, Hallelujah,'" but it is not known who adapted the tune to Mrs. Howe's poem nor if she actually had the "favorite melody" in mind as a setting when she wrote the poem. The song has been known and used (with various intentions) by generations of soldiers, school children, politicians and church choirs and by numerous musicians as varied as Max Steiner, Charles Ives, Mahalia Jackson and Judy Garland.

Beautiful River

Robert Lowry (1826–1899) wrote both text and music of this famous gospel song which has long been known by its opening line, "Shall we gather at the river." It was apparently the extreme heat of a July afternoon in 1864 that induced a kind of reverie in Rev. Lowry, at the time minister of the Hanson Place Baptist Church in Brooklyn. He got an image of the Apocalypse in the Book of Revelations: "Brightest of all were the throne," he later wrote, "the heavenly river, and the gathering of the saints." With this in mind, he composed "Beautiful River." Lowry wrote a number of popular gospel and secular pieces, including "All the Way My Saviour Leads Me," "I Need Thee Every Hour" and "Where Is My Boy Tonight." In the late 1860s he became associated with the successful New York music publishers Biglow and Main and edited Sunday-school collections with titles such as *Bright Jewels, Good As Gold* and *Joyful Lays.*

In 1865 the Brooklyn Sunday School Union used "Beautiful River" and forty thousand children sang it on parade in the streets of Brooklyn. Its first publication was in that year in the collection *Happy Voices* (New York, The American Tract Society). In the collection the piece is printed in the usual hymnbook style on two staves, the verse section in three parts and the chorus in four. In the first sheet-music edition (1866), reproduced here—the cover engraving of the beautiful river has sailboats instead of Lowry's saints—there is a separate keyboard accompaniment for piano or melodeon (a small reed organ) arranged by E. Mack. The verse is a duet for soprano and alto and the chorus is in four parts. It also has an additional verse (the third) not present in *Happy Voices.*

Lowry apparently was not especially proud of the piece that became his most famous creation. Ira D. Sankey quoted him as saying: "It is brass-band music, has a march movement, and for that reason became popular, though, for myself, I do not think much of it" (Sankey, p. 68; see Bibliography).

Ben Bolt

Philadelphia-born Thomas Dunn English (1819–1902) had a long and varied career. He had degrees in medicine and law; he was the author of plays, articles and quantities of verse; he was the editor of various journals; and, late in life, he was a member of the U.S. House of Representatives for two terms (1891–95). It was writing, however, that he pursued most ardently, though without any substantial success. His reputation was more or less that of tireless amateur and dabbler. At one time, his friend Edgar Allan Poe spoofed him in a published article as a dilettante; English in turn accused Poe of plagiarism. Poe sued for libel and won. English's modest literary fame rests upon one poem, "Ben Bolt," which he produced when Nathaniel P. Willis requested a piece for *The New Mirror*, a New York weekly newspaper edited by Willis and George P. Morris (author of "Woodman! Spare That Tree!"). The poem was first published in the issue of September 2, 1843.

Many songwriters eventually set *Ben Bolt* to music, but the only version to gain real popularity was that of Nelson F. Kneass (1825–1868), who made his setting in Pittsburgh in 1848. There is some reason to believe, however, that Kneass—a singer and black-face minstrel—merely adapted an existing tune instead of composing an original one. Along with other writers, William S. Hunt stated that Kneass used a German melody as the basis for his setting, though *which* melody is not known. In a detailed 1933 article, "The Story of a Song" (see Bibliography), Hunt claims that Kneass was basically unmusical, that for him "the art of creative composition was almost an impossibility" (Hunt, p. 30). An earlier charge involving plagiarism was also made against Kneass. Robert Peebles Nevin reported in the article "Stephen C. Foster and Negro Minstrelsy" (*Atlantic Monthly*, November 1867) that Kneass (in the same year he set "Ben Bolt") had attempted to register for copyright as his own work the Foster song "Away Down South," only to be intercepted by Morrison Foster arriving at the Pittsburgh registrar's office on the same mission for his brother. (Kneass, as singer, had participated in the first public performance of the Foster song before it was published, as he had in that of "Oh! Susanna" a year earlier.) In defense of Kneass it must be recalled that he is credited with a number of published songs other than "Ben Bolt," among them "I Hear the Hoofs on the Hill" (1849), "Poor Aunt Dinah" (1850), "Gently Down the Stream" (1854) and "My Canoe is on the Ohio" (1854). Questions of the originality of Kneass's "Ben Bolt" aside, it is the one that swept to fame over many competitive versions. He must be credited, after all, with crafting one of the most famous songs of the era.

Forty-six years after the appearance of "Ben Bolt" it enjoyed a great new wave of popularity with the publication of George Du Maurier's novel *Trilby* (1894). In this best-selling tale of the mad genius Svengali who mesmerizes his unmusical protégée Trilby O'Ferrall into a great singer, "Ben Bolt" was used almost as a kind of "Dies Irae" motif. It is the song that Trilby is to sing at her London debut, at the climax of the novel, when Svengali dies of a heart attack and the protégée reverts to her tone-deaf state, her singing voice evaporated. Early in the book, "Ben Bolt" is planted as an item of portent when it is woven in and around the first meeting of Trilby and Svengali. In a "double improvisation" by Svengali at the piano and Gecko, his henchman-companion, on the violin, it rises to a state of absurd glorification. Here is Du Maurier's ecstatic description of the performance:

> [They] played that simple melody as it had probably never been played before—such passion, such pathos, such tone!—and they turned it and twisted it, and went from one key to another, playing into each other's hands, Svengali taking the lead; and fugued and canoned and counterpointed and battledored and shuttlecocked it, high and low, soft and loud, in minor, in pizzicato, and in sordino—adagio, andante, allegretto, scherzo—and exhausted all its possibilities of beauty . . . and the masterful Ben Bolt . . . [was] magnified into a strange, almost holy poetic dignity and splendor quite undreamed of by whoever wrote the words and music of that unsophisticated little song, which has touched so many simple British hearts that don't know any better . . . (*Trilby*, London, J. M. Dent & Sons, 1931, pp. 20–22).

The year after the publication of *Trilby*, it was dramatized by Paul Potter, with the heroine's aborted performance of "Ben Bolt" as climax. Both the novel and the play were immensely successful in America, and the firm of S. Brainard's Sons Company of Chicago immediately issued "Ben Bolt" in a "Trilby Edition" (1895) with a two-color title page and a drawing of the mesmerized singer. Numerous revivals of the play in the twentieth century have contributed to the perpetuation of the song. It has also been used in several films, most memorably perhaps in *Gone With the Wind* (Vivien Leigh as Scarlett sings snatches of "Ben Bolt" most charmingly in the famous bedroom scene on the morning after Rhett has asserted his sexual rights as husband of that willful Southern lady). Thus the little memento mori of the 1840s, the casual creation of the Philadelphia poetaster and the Pittsburgh minstrel, sailed securely into modern times, so securely, in fact, that in 1955 the historian Gilbert Chase could refer to it with some exasperation (though not without a touch of backhanded compliment) as "one of those moribund songs that refuse to die" (Chase, p. 290; see Bibliography).

The Bonnie Blue Flag

If "Dixie" was the Confederacy's national anthem, "The Bonnie Blue Flag" was its marching song. The tune used for this song is an Irish folk air, "The Irish Jaunting Car," and the text was by Harry Macarthy, an English singer and songwriter. Macarthy apparently fashioned the piece for his own performance while touring the South early in 1861. He blatantly exploited the secession fever on the eve of the war and created the desired sensation. His use of the flag as dominant image followed a sure-fire international wartime tradition and greatly enhanced the song's appeal. The main business of the piece, occupying verses three through six, is a roll call of the seceded states; at the finish "The Single Star of the Bonnie Blue Flag has grown to be Eleven."

Commentators and historians have long noted the paucity of effective native Confederate war songs. Dozens of songs were written by Southerners during the war but none seemed capable of capturing the collective public imagination with the kind of power—patriotic, propagandistic or spiritual—that blazed in the works of George F. Root, Henry Clay Work, Julia Ward Howe, Walter Kittredge or even Stephen Foster in one or two of his war songs. The three songs most used by the Confederates, and which are most associated with their cause, were all borrowed goods: "Dixie," from the New York minstrel stage; "Maryland, My Maryland!," which used a German folk tune; and the Irish-English "Bonnie Blue Flag."

Some Southerners were well aware that the North had all the best songs and after the war some of them said so; *The Century* magazine quoted a Confederate major, speaking to some Union officers, shortly after Lee's surrender: "Gentlemen, if we'd had your songs we'd have whipped you out of your boots! Who couldn't have marched or fought with such songs? We had nothing, absolutely nothing, except a bastard 'Marseillaise,' the 'Bonny Blue Flag' and 'Dixie,' which are nothing but jigs. 'Maryland, My Maryland' was a splendid song, but [it] was about as inspiring as the 'Dead March in Saul' . . ." (quoted in Root's *The Story of a Musical Life*, p. 135; see Bibliography).

Camptown Races

Many of the songs popular in nineteenth-century America are of course still known, but there is undoubtedly only one *composer* of such songs who has remained widely famous in the present century: Stephen Collins Foster (1826–1864). Five of his best-known songs are included in this collection. "Camptown Races" was composed probably in 1849 in Cincinnati and was published by F. D. Benteen of Baltimore in February 1850. As can be seen from the original title page, the song was released as "Gwine to Run All Night, or De Camptown Races." It was the latter phrase, however, that rapidly caught the public's imagination and became the popular title. As soon as 1852, Benteen published a second edition of the song, this time with guitar accompaniment and a title page that read: "The celebrated Ethiopian Song/Camptown Races." The song's dialect verses have all the wild exaggeration and rough charm of a real folk tale as well as some of Foster's most vivid imagery:

> Old muley cow come on to de track . . .
> De bob-tail fling her ober his back . . .
> Den fly along like a rail-road car . . .
> Runnin' a race wid a shootin' star . . .

Foster quite carefully tailored the song for use on the minstrel stage. He composed it as a piece for solo voice with group interjections and refrain; he marked the score specifically:

> SOLO
> Camptown ladies sing dis song
> CHORUS
> Doo-dah! doo-dah!
> SOLO
> De Camptown racetrack five miles long
> CHORUS
> Oh doo-dah day!
> etc.

The tune is an ideal vehicle for syncopated banjo parts with a rhythm section of tambourines and rattling bones. Together with "Oh! Susanna," "Camptown Races" is one of the gems of the minstrel era.

Carry Me Back to Old Virginny

As Stephen Foster and Daniel Emmett are the most memorable composers of American minstrelsy's Golden Era from the 1840s to the 1860s, James A. Bland (1854–1911) is the stellar talent of its latter days in the 1870s and '80s. This black composer reputedly wrote a great number of songs—most sources say as many as seven hundred—but apparently only a relatively small number are known to have survived. He is remembered chiefly for three pieces: "Carry Me Back to Old Virginny," "Oh, Dem Golden Slippers" and "In the Evening by the Moonlight," all of which are in this collection. The first-named song is certainly his most famous. In a 1939 article on Bland (see Bibliography), Kelly Miller states that it was composed in 1875; it was copyrighted in 1878 and, like most of his songs, was composed for the minstrel stage.

"Carry Me Back" is clear evidence that Bland was well acquainted with the stereotypes of the so-called "plantation melodies," for in its expression of a misplaced "darkey's" longing for an old Southern home it follows a successful formula that was already established when Stephen Foster composed "Old Folks at Home" in 1851. Bland's ex-Virginian stands easily beside his aging prewar relatives who yearned for the Swanee River and who wished to be in the land of cotton to live and die in Dixie. Apparently not even the catastrophic intervention of the Civil War and the changing social climate could totally alter the conventions of the minstrel show. This tenacious institution could not, however, face the twentieth century; by the time of Bland's death in 1911 it had all but faded from the scene.

Long after the minstrel show—and this black composer himself—were safely interred, the legislature of Virginia could proclaim the old favorite the official state song in 1940. It did have to be "corrected," however, no doubt to avoid unnecessary reminders of its minstrel past; thus it was adopted, dialect expunged, as "Carry Me Back to Old Virginia." For further biographical data on Bland, see the note on "In the Evening by the Moonlight."

Champagne Charlie

In the mid-1860s, Joe Saunders, a mechanic and singer from the Midlands of England, was brought to London and launched on a theatrical career by the impresario Charles Roberts. His name was changed to George Leybourne, and he became one of the leading performers in the early English music hall. Leybourne developed as his stage persona the so-called Heavy Swell, which was a caricature of the fashionable dandies of London society. He crystallized this character with the song "Champagne Charlie" (1867) and it brought him instant fame. The English writer Archibald Haddon (see Bibliography) described a characteristic performance: "In a puce jacket, a brilliantly-coloured vest, and trousers either enormously checked or striped like railway-lines, George Leybourne led [the] chorus: 'Champagne Charley is my name . . . Good for any game at night—boys! So, who'll come and join me in a spree?'"

Leybourne's manager encouraged him to maintain his theatrical image off stage as well as on and provided him with a carriage drawn by four white horses to take him to and from the theater. The one-time mechanic, reportedly a tall and handsome figure, maintained an elegant wardrobe and, like his character Charlie, became an inveterate drinker of champagne. As careers go in the theater, his was a fairly long one—just under twenty years—but he was only 42 when he died in 1884.

"Champagne Charlie" was only one of numerous vehicles composed especially for Leybourne by the prolific English songwriter Alfred Lee. Leybourne is credited in the published song as author of the lyrics, as he was in several others, but this cannot be taken without question. It was a common practice of the time for performers to attach their names to their successful numbers, so it is quite possible that Lee was solely responsible for this and other of their supposedly joint creations.

"Champagne Charlie" apparently crossed the Atlantic immediately; several American editions appeared in quick succession. It was published by Ditson of Boston in 1867 (the year Leybourne introduced it in London), with a totally new text by one H. J. Whymark under the title "Champagne Charlie Was His Name," and by William Hall of New York in 1868 with yet another text by the prolific George Cooper. Also around this time Lee & Walker of Philadelphia brought out the song in a handsome edition with the full British text as it had originally appeared; this is the version chosen for the present volume. "Charlie" was obviously a hot property, and it succeeded here apparently without benefit of George Leybourne's sparkling presence to promote it; there seems to be no evidence that he ever performed in America.

Darling Nelly Gray

From a reported total of about eighty songs composed by Benjamin Russel Hanby (1833–1867), the Ohio teacher-minister-songwriter, four achieved wide popularity: "Ole Shady or The Song of the Contraband," an early Civil War song; "Santa Claus" (or "Up on the Housetop," 1864), a children's Christmas song; "Who Is He in Yonder Stall?" (1866), a Protestant hymn; and "Darling Nelly Gray" (1856), his first and greatest success. The opening verses of the famous "Nelly Gray," with their images of an old Kentucky shore, a little red canoe and a banjo sweetly played, suggest yet another pleasant, if conventional, mid-century ballad intended perhaps for the minstrel stage. The chorus's "they," who have taken Nelly away, does not become ominous until the third verse. Here the propagandist heart of the piece is revealed, the reason that led it to be called "the Uncle Tom's Cabin of Song," for "Nelly" was intended as fuel for the abolitionists' fire: "The white man bound her with his chain, They have taken her to Georgia for to wear her life away . . . ." As with characters in *Uncle Tom's Cabin*, the song's hero and heroine find satisfaction only in death. (Incidentally, the song's influence and popularity must have reached Stephen Foster, whose "Old Black Joe" four years later echoed: "I'm coming, I'm coming . . . I hear the angel voices calling . . . .")

There is a fairly elaborate story about the background of the song and the real-life prototypes of the characters; it involves a runaway slave named Joseph Selby who died at the home of Hanby's father while on his way to Canada to earn money to buy the freedom of his lover named, yes, Nelly Gray. A detailed account of the story and of Hanby's brief career and family background can be found in, of all places, the *Congressional Record* (89th Congress, First Session, 1965). It is a long address by Judge Earl R. Hoover entitled "Benjamin R. Hanby—'The Stephen Foster of Ohio'" and was appended to the *Record* by Representative Clarence Brown of Ohio.

Der Deitcher's Dog

"Der Deitcher's Dog" (1864) is one of three songs in this collection by Septimus Winner (1827–1902); the others are "Listen to the Mocking Bird" and "Whispering Hope," both issued under the name Alice Hawthorne, one of Winner's several pseudonyms. The composer was a native and lifelong resident of Philadelphia and came from a family that included a violin maker (his father, Joseph Eastburn Winner), a portrait painter (his uncle, William E. Winner) and one other songwriter (his brother, Joseph E. Winner, composer of "The Little Brown Jug," which is also included in this collection). As a young husband and father (he married at twenty), Septimus earned a meager living in the late 1840s as a free-lance violinist, shopkeeper and music teacher, offering instruction in the violin and other instruments. His fortunes began to improve when he turned to songwriting in the 1850s, rose considerably after he became his own publisher, and settled to a comfortable plateau with a long series of popular instrument instruction manuals brought out by Oliver Ditson, the large Boston music house.

Winner's "Comic Ballad" of 1864, perhaps most usually remembered as "Oh Where, Oh Where Has My Little Dog Gone," indicates that he was acquainted with members of Philadelphia's large German community. The rather crude dialect text is original, but the melody is borrowed (without acknowledgment) from the German folksong "Lauterbach," which is about a young man losing a stocking and his heart in Lauterbach, and begins:

> Z'Lauterbach han i mein Strumpf verlor'n,
> Ohne Strumpf gang i net hoam!

The song's "Tra-la-la" chorus, a Bavarian yodel that evokes an oom-pah-pah beer-garden band, is amusing, but it cannot quite dispel the grim black comedy of the last verse with its suggestion that the missing dog has been turned into sausage.

Dixie's Land

As might be expected of one of America's most famous songs—one that was so intimately bound up with an important era in American history—"Dixie" has been the subject of extensive study. Writers have explored all aspects of the song—the circumstances of its creation, the rather complicated history of its publication, the biography of its composer, the background and meaning of the word Dixie, etc.—to the extent that it has its own little body of literature. The single most comprehensive investigation of the song is in Hans Nathan's excellent study *Dan Emmett and the Rise of Early Negro Minstrelsy* (see Bibliography). "Dixie" is actually a kind of slang title by which the piece came to be known. The text first appeared under the title "Dixie's Land" (in an 1859 songster published in New York) and the song itself was published with "I Wish I Was in Dixie's Land" on the cover. The author of both text and music was of course Daniel Decatur Emmett, the Ohio-born pioneer minstrel performer and composer whose lifetime spanned almost a century, from 1815 to 1904. Emmett was with Bryant's Minstrels in New York from 1858 to 1866, serving as singer, violinist and resident composer, and it was for this troupe that he composed "Dixie" in 1859.

The song became a hit but for some reason was not immediately published in New York; it traveled to New Orleans first and was published there in a pirated edition early in 1860 by P. P. Werlein without mention of Emmett. The first authorized edition was published in June of that year by Firth, Pond & Co. in New York. Its early appearance in New Orleans was no doubt an important factor in its rapid and widespread popularity throughout the South. After the outbreak of the Civil War, "Dixie" somehow became synonymous with the Confederacy. It became the unofficial national anthem and a great battle cry for those who would take their stand "to lib an die in Dixie."

Down in Alabam'

Bryant's Minstrels, for whom Emmett wrote "Dixie," were the most prominent New York troupe following the great heyday of Edwin P. Christy. It was run by three brothers—Dan, Jerry and Neil Bryant—who were also the stars of the troupe, and it operated in one form or another from 1857 into the 1870s. In *Dan Emmett and the Rise of Early Negro Minstrelsy*, Hans Nathan discusses the innovations brought to the minstrel format by the Bryants, especially in regard to the closing section of the shows known as the walk-around. Until the Bryants, this section was a dance to instrumental music, performed as a solo in earlier days and, later on, by a small group or the whole ensemble. The Bryants introduced singing into the walk-around. Two or three lead performers at the front of the stage would sing solo stanzas of a song, with the company behind them in a semicircle making interjections and clapping in rhythm. All joined in the final chorus, with the lead performers dancing in a circle to the concluding instrumental passages. As Nathan points out, this kind of pattern had definite parallels to the performance of both religious "shouts" and secular music by plantation Negroes: the element of solo and response singing, the circular movements, the rhythmic clapping.

One of the earliest of the Bryants' walk-arounds after they opened in February 1857 was entitled "Plantation Song and Dance, or Southern Life, Down in Alabama." The song used here must certainly have been "Down in Alabam', or Aint I Glad I Got Out de Wilderness" (copyrighted early in 1858). The form of the song is unusual and seems tailored especially for the pattern of the Bryants' walk-around. It begins with a lively eight-measure instrumental introduction setting the piece's basic polka rhythm; the next section is a series of syncopated instrumental "snaps" interspersed with vocal "Ah's!" which the score indicates are to be sung by "All the voices"; the verse section follows, marked "Solo"; the chorus is for three solo voices—the three leads of the walk-around—with a heavy accent on each appearance of the word "out"; at the end of the chorus is the direction "Go back to Symphony," which means that the piece will eventually conclude with the instrumental opening music (probably in extended form) for the final dance. This walk-around has more than a casual connection with black Southern religious music. It appears to be based on, or derived from the same common source as, the old slave hymn "Go in the Wilderness" which appears in *Slave Songs of the United States* (New York, 1867), the first published collection of Negro spirituals. The melody of "Down in Alabam'" and the germ of the text are found in the concluding lines of the spiritual. The published sheet music of "Alabam'" credits the words and music to a J. Warner about whom no information has been located.

This song, of course, was eventually transformed and became known as "The Old Gray Mare," but apparently it was not until the twentieth century that the familiar text, beginning "The old gray mare she ain't what she used to be," appeared in published form.

The Flying Trapeze

In a delightful sequence in Frank Capra's 1934 film *It Happened One Night*, Clark Gable and Claudette Colbert lead their fellow passengers on a cross-country bus in a rousing performance of the old favorite "The Flying Trapeze." The distance between a London music hall of 1867 and a Hollywood movie studio of 1934 is considerable, but "The Flying Trapeze" survived the journey with the greatest of ease, its charm intact.

The song was first published in London in 1867 or 1868 and was introduced by George Leybourne, the early music-hall star who became famous with "Champagne Charlie." The credits in the published music read "Written by George Leybourne" and "Arranged by Alfred Lee," but as in the case of "Champagne Charlie" it is not unlikely that the song was solely the work of Alfred Lee. Though the catalogues of the British Museum contain upwards of one hundred titles of songs and arrangements by Lee (dating from the late 1860s to the early 1890s), some of which were very popular on both sides of the Atlantic, no biographical information seems to have found its way into British or American reference books.

It is known, however, that the songwriters associated with British music hall during Alfred Lee's time generally did not have an easy time financially. Songs were written for individual performers and sold outright to publishers for a flat sum, and though pieces such as "The Flying Trapeze" became immensely popular and sold thousands of copies in sheet music, the composers received no royalty payments. Lee and his fellow British songwriters were further exploited by American publishers who could pirate their work at will without payments of any kind. Until the first International Copyright Law was enacted by Congress in 1891, no foreign publication could be copyrighted in the United States; such material was considered in the public domain and any publisher who wished could issue it. Thus in the case of European successes such as "The Flying Trapeze" and "Champagne Charlie," editions were brought out practically simultaneously by publishers in New York, Philadelphia, Boston and San Francisco. Alfred Lee may or may not have appreciated the backhanded compliment.

Goober Peas

This is an anonymous Confederate soldier song that originated and was popular during the Civil War but apparently was not published until 1866. It is of course a reflection of the increasingly scanty diet of the Southern troops as the war moved to its conclusion. It was a time when the plentiful Georgia peanut (or goober pea) could be an important supplement to dwindling rations. Note the "composer's" name "P. Nutt."

Grandfather's Clock

After the prosperous firm of Root & Cady was forced out of business by the great Chicago fire of October 1871, Chauncey M. Cady (1824–1889) eventually moved to New York and started his own music publishing house around 1875. The new company, C. M. Cady, located at 107 Duane Street, lasted only five years, but it produced one stunning success. Cady persuaded his old Chicago friend Henry Clay Work, who had been responsible for so many of Root & Cady's best-selling war songs and parlor ballads, to quit his temporary retirement from songwriting and work up material for the New York house. Among the songs Work submitted was "Grandfather's Clock," which he had composed several years earlier. It was published by Cady in 1876 and became popular at once; it reputedly sold about 800,000 copies in the United States and earned four thousand dollars in royalties for Work. The song is still beguiling in its simplicity, naturalness, humor and the easy flow of melody and accompaniment. The composer of "Kingdom Coming" had returned in fine form, his technique even surer and more refined.

Home! Sweet Home!

This Anglo-American product of 1823 could easily compete as the most famous song of the nineteenth century on a worldwide basis. It is one of those genteel, vaguely "classical," pieces that have achieved popularity of quite phenomenal dimensions. The music for "Home! Sweet Home!" was composed by Henry Rowley Bishop (1786-1855), an English conductor and composer prominent in the opera and concert life of his day. He composed over 130 light operas and other stage works and was associated for years with Covent Garden, the leading opera house of London. Though "Home! Sweet Home!" was Bishop's most famous piece, it was perhaps not representative of his own sentiments: he has been described as "a noted reprobate, home-wrecker and spendthrift; and he died in poverty" (Turner, p. 144; see Bibliography). *Grove's Dictionary*, however, remarks that his songs are "remembered with affection for such qualities as they have. 'Home, sweet home' . . . still remains a good tune."

Bishop's collaborator was the colorful American writer-actor-diplomat John Howard Payne (1791–1852). After a taste of early but short-lived success in the New York theater—at fifteen his first play was staged and at eighteen he made an impression performing as a handsome juvenile—he went to Europe and shuttled between London and Paris for about twenty years. He authored a number of large, ambitious, unsuccessful plays and was, in general, a failure at just about everything he attempted, including a love affair with Mary Wollstonecraft Shelley. He enjoyed the friendship and support of Washington Irving and had an occasional modest success, but he was apparently always near poverty and always in debt (he even served a sentence in debtor's prison). After another period of ten years in the United States, Payne was a somewhat famous figure and managed to obtain from President Tyler in 1842 the post of American consul at Tunis. He died there at age 61.

By and large, Payne's "slender immortality" (to quote the *Dictionary of American Biography*) is based upon his authorship of "Home! Sweet Home!" He wrote the lyric for the libretto he adapted from his play *Clari, or The Maid of Milan*. In the reference books, *Clari* is invariably referred to as an opera, presumably because in 1823 this is what it and other such works were routinely labeled. In the twentieth century, however, it would be considered an operetta or play with music. "Home! Sweet Home!" is sung by Clari at her first entrance in Act I and is heard several times throughout the play. The peasant heroine has been more or less abducted from her childhood home (which seems to be in a suburb of Milan) by the dashing Duke Vivaldi, who has promised her marriage and nobility but clearly has other plans once she is safely locked in his castle. Much of the action consists of Clari ungratefully resisting the Duke, rejecting his gifts, crying a good deal, and singing "Home! Sweet Home!" Comic relief is provided by two servants, Vespina and Jocoso, with the second act given over largely to a curious divertissement in the form of a *Hamlet*-like play-within-a-play in which the story of Clari and the Duke is reenacted by a group of strolling players to no discernible dramatic purpose. There is a happy ending after Clari breaks through the castle's apparently feeble security system, walks back to her village, confronts her parents who forgive her for permitting herself to be abducted, and is finally united with the now conscience-stricken Duke amid the cheers of the villagers. *Clari* was the hit of London's 1823 spring season and "Home! Sweet Home!" went around the world.

I'll Take You Home Again, Kathleen

Perusing the literature of "stories" of old popular songs can be both frustrating and amusing. One finds widely divergent accounts of how, when and where a particular song came to be written, conflicting reports on the places and dates of birth and death of composers and poets, and disagreement on when, where and by whom a song was first published. There can scarcely be many other bodies of "nonfiction" on a single subject so riddled with casual scholarship (where it is present at all) and heady whimsicality. The search for hard facts among the writings is perilous. Many authors seem especially bent on creating, perpetuating or elaborating upon supposedly real-life dramas surrounding the creation of certain songs; ideally such scenarios must be rich with colorful characters, humor, pathos and, best of all, a touch of tragedy, all to invest the songs with a certain dimension and importance, to render their texts pregnant with subtle meaning. "I'll Take You Home Again, Kathleen," by Thomas P. Westendorf (1848?-1923), provides an excellent example of a famous song about which there exist not only conflicting reports of names, dates and places but also a whole clutch of tear-stained dramas of its creation. After surveying several sources on "Kathleen," one is left with a number of questions, of which the following are only a sample:

1. Was the song composed and/or published in 1875, 1876 or 1900?

2. Was it composed in Louisville, Kentucky, or on a ship in the middle of the Atlantic Ocean?

3. Was the composer inspired to write the song

when his wife, ill and bereaved over the death of their young son, asked him to take her from their home in Louisville to visit her old family home in New York? Or was he inspired by his wife's asking him to take her back home to Bowling Green, Virginia, while they were touring Europe in an attempt to recover from the death of their son?

4. Was Westendorf's wife named Kathleen, Jane or Jennie? Or was she called Kathleen as a nickname by her husband though her real name was Jane? Did she really die of a broken heart on shipboard, and was she buried at sea?

Though "Kathleen" continues to float in a sea of a different kind—that of misinformation—she was actually rescued in 1948 by the librarian-scholar Richard J. Hill, though some writers are apparently unaware of this act of mercy. In *Notes* (June 1948), the journal of the Music Library Association, Hill presented the history of the song in a fifteen-page article entitled "Getting Kathleen Home Again" that derived from exhaustive research in the copyright files at The Library of Congress, city directories and correspondence with other researchers and surviving friends and relatives of the Westendorf family. Here are the answers he provided to the above questions:

1. The song was written in the late fall of 1875 and first published in the March 1876 issue of *Church's Musical Visitor*, the house organ of John Church & Co., Cincinnati.

2. It was written neither in Louisville nor on the Atlantic but in Plainfield, Indiana, while Westendorf was a teacher and music instructor at a school for delinquent boys (his main profession). The Westendorfs never went to Europe.

3. He wrote "Kathleen" as an "answer" to a song entitled "Barney, Take Me Home Again" (published in November 1875) by his friend and frequent collaborator George W. Persley (not Parsely as some writers have it). At the time the song was written Mrs. Westendorf was on a trip to her family home in Ogdensburg, New York, but this had nothing to do with the origin of the song. The Westendorfs did lose a son later in their marriage, but again, this had no bearing on the song's genesis.

4. Mrs. Westendorf's name was Jennie and she was not called Kathleen by her husband or anyone else. She died in Memphis in 1915.

In the Evening by the Moonlight

James A. Bland was one of relatively few black composers and entertainers who had a highly successful career in the minstrel business. He was born in 1854 in Flushing (now part of New York City) and spent most of his youth in Washington, D.C. He was for a time a page in the House of Representatives and he attended Howard University, graduating in 1873. His talents as singer and especially as songwriter led him to try for a theatrical career, and by the mid-1870s he was composing for and performing with various all-Negro minstrel troupes. Such groups were not uncommon after the Civil War and vied successfully with the white shows, adopting the old minstrel-show conventions—even wearing burnt-cork makeup—and adding new twists.

The cover of "In the Evening by the Moonlight" (copyrighted 1880) bills Bland as "The Best Ethiopian Song Writer in the World." It was probably composed while he was a member of Jack Haverly's All Colored Troupe, which performed in New York and toured the country as far as the Pacific coast. Haverly managed more than one troupe and he worked all sorts of innovations into their formats: he assembled huge casts (including both men and women) of singers, dancers and comedians; he featured elaborate costumes, specialty acts and even orchestras. Gone were the days of Christy and Bryant; vaudeville, burlesque and musical comedy were on the rise.

In 1881 Haverly introduced his All Colored Troupe to London with great success. It was a significant event for Bland: he apparently found England congenial and the prospects for a black performer and songwriter promising. He eventually left Haverly and lived in England for the better part of twenty years. Despite his considerable success abroad he returned to America after the turn of the century, the minstrel business now in eclipse. He made one attempt to enter the new world of show business with the score of a musical entitled *The Sporting Girl*, but it was not successful when performed in Washington. He eventually moved to Philadelphia and died there of tuberculosis in 1911.

Jim Crack Corn (or The Blue Tail Fly)

"De Blue Tail Fly" was a song apparently used by the Virginia Minstrels, the famous short-lived original minstrel band organized by Daniel Emmett and three friends in 1843 (the group is discussed in the notes for "Old Dan Tucker"). It was first published by Keith's of Boston in 1844 as part of *Old Dan Emmit's*[*sic*] *Original Banjo Melodies* (second series), though it is not known whether Emmett actually wrote it. The song survives, however, in another anonymous, slightly later, version as "Jim Crack Corn, or The Blue Tail Fly." The seven verses of this version are almost identical to verses three through nine of the original ten-verse song, but the music is entirely different. Also, the original did not have a vocal chorus section and did not include the lines "Jim crack corn I don't care . . . Ole Massa gone away." In the 1846 edition reprinted here, the Baltimore publisher F. D. Benteen exploited the name of the Virginia Minstrels though they had disbanded about two years before, and may never have used this version.

John Lair reports in his *Songs Lincoln Loved* (see Bibliography) that "De Blue Tail Fly" was Lincoln's favorite minstrel piece; he called it "that buzzing song."

Jingle Bells

In 1857 Oliver Ditson of Boston issued a song entitled "The One Horse Open Sleigh" by a J. Pierpont; except for the usual scrollwork lettering, the song's cover was plain; it sold for 25 cents a copy. In 1859 Ditson issued the same song as "Jingle Bells, Or the One horse open Sleigh;" it had a cover decorated with a large collar of sleigh bells and it sold for thirty cents. During the intervening two years the song had apparently caught the public's fancy because of the charming chorus with the jingling bells, and Ditson went to the expense of engraving totally new plates to exploit this appeal. (The case is similar to that of Foster's "Camptown Races," issued first as "Gwine to Run All Night.") Curiously enough, it is the famous jingle-bell chorus that eventually was somehow transformed by popular use into a totally different tune, while the verse section remained virtually intact as originally published.

The composer, James Pierpont (1822–1893), was from a large and interesting family. He was one of the six children of the formidable John Pierpont (1785–1886), a famous figure on the East coast for many years, who had degrees from both Yale College and Harvard Divinity School and was a published poet, a widely admired lecturer, an enthusiast of phrenology and spiritualism, a fiery reformer and a Unitarian minister. John was also the grandfather (and James the uncle) of J. P. (for Pierpont) Morgan. A high point of John's career was the battle waged with his Boston congregation because of his views as an abolitionist and especially as an advocate of temperance. The congregation withheld his salary and attacked his character, but a church court ruled in his favor. The victor, he collected his back pay—and resigned.

A fair amount has been written about John Pierpont, including a lengthy article in the *Dictionary of American Biography*, but very little about James (he is not even mentioned in the *Dictionary*). According to an article by Frank W. Lovering (see Bibliography), he was something of a wanderer. He reputedly wrote "Jingle Bells" in 1850 in Medford, Massachusetts, where his father had a church after the Boston episode. By this time James apparently had already worked as a seaman and lived in San Francisco. He eventually married twice and fathered five children. His father lived to see him take up residence in the South and espouse the Conferedate cause as composer of such songs as "We Conquer or Die" (1861), which makes reference to "Northern bigots," and "Strike for the South" (1863). He spent his later years in Winter Haven, Florida, and died there at age 71. His biggest success as a songwriter during his lifetime was not "Jingle Bells" (its worldwide familiarity seems to be a twentieth-century phenomenon) but rather a ballad entitled "The Little White Cottage, or Gentle Nettie Moore" published in 1857, the same year as "The One Horse Open Sleigh."

Johnny Get Your Gun

In a late-nineteenth-century newspaper article headlined "Local Song Writers/Brooklyn People Have Made Fame and Some Money by Their Compositions" (in the Clipping File of the Music Division, The New York Public Library), Monroe H. Rosenfeld (1861–1918) is described as "a wide awake young man of highly sensitive and nervous temperament, and a schooled musician." He is perhaps the stellar talent among the Brooklynites in the field: "His songs usually command his own figure, which varies from $50 to $300. One of his songs alone has reached the phenomenal sale of over a hundred thousand copies, paying him several thousand dollars in royalties. Mr. Rosenfeld first became known under the *nom de plume* of 'F. Heiser' and 'F. Belasco.'" It was under the latter name that T. B. Harms published Rosenfeld's popular minstrel piece of 1886, "Johnny Get Your Gun." The song itself, however, did not prove to be a long-lasting favorite: it was the sixteen-bar "Dance" that concludes the piece that remained familiar. This was undoubtedly due to the fact that George M. Cohan (1878–1942) borrowed the tune for the verse of his World War I classic "Over There" (1917). Furthermore, he used Rosenfeld's title in the text:

> Johnny get your gun, get your gun . . .
> Take it on the run, on the run . . .

Rosenfeld was alive to hear his 31-year-old minstrel piece in its new transformation, but his reaction apparently was not recorded. The phrase "Johnny get your gun" could perhaps be considered a venerable common property and available for anyone's use—it appears in at least one folksong (see *The New Lost City Ramblers Song Book*, New York, Oak Publications, 1964, p. 214)—but the familiar little tune that matches the phrase was certainly Rosenfeld's original. Both phrase and tune were borrowed one other time, ten years after "Over There," for the song "Tin Pan Parade" (1927) by Haven Gillespie and Richard A. Whiting; here they were also used as the beginning of the verse, as in the Cohan song—the quotation of a quotation. And of course the phrase was used—with a twist—to create the title of one of Irving Berlin's most famous shows, *Annie Get Your Gun.*

Just Before the Battle, Mother

This was another of George F. Root's contributions to the war effort, though it must have proved small comfort to anxious Civil War mothers with sons on the battlefield. Nevertheless, the song became widely popular after it was published in 1864. In it Root shrewdly combines the older conventions of the "home" song and the "mother" song with the currently topical theme of death on the battlefield. It proved to be a surefire combination: everyone could weep indulgently at their parlor pianos and feel that they were somehow serving a noble cause. Root was only one of many songwriters who worked the formula with success, and he himself worked it several times. The third verse of "Just Before the Battle, Mother" contains a blatant plug for Root's earlier battle song ("Hear the 'Battle-Cry of Freedom' "). He justifies this with the footnote at the bottom of the page.

Kingdom Coming

George F. Root, represented by three songs in this collection, "discovered" the composer of "Kingdom Coming" and other nineteenth-century popular classics. In his autobiography Root tells of his first meeting with Henry Clay Work (1832–1884):

> One day early in the war a quiet and rather solemn-looking young man, poorly clad, was sent up to my room from the store [Root & Cady] with a song for me to examine. I looked at it and then at him in astonishment. It was "Kingdom Coming," —elegant in manuscript, full of bright, good sense and comical situations in its "darkey" dialect—the words fitting the melody almost as aptly and neatly as Gilbert fits Sullivan—the melody decidedly good and taking, and the whole exactly suited to the times. . . . He needed some musical help that I could give him, and we needed just such songs as he could write. The connection, which continued some years, proved very profitable both to him and to us . . . .

"Kingdom Coming" was introduced by Christy's Minstrels in Chicago with much promotional fanfare in April 1862; it was published the next month and quickly spread far beyond Chicago. The events pictured in the song, casually referred to by Root as "comical situations," are grim and bitterly satiric. Work was not unacquainted with the realities of slave life: his abolitionist father was an active participant in helping runaway slaves on the Underground Railroad and their home in Illinois was a "station"; the father served a jail sentence for his activities. The great tune itself, perfectly fit for a jubilee and one of the most memorable of the era, creates a double edge to the satire. How far removed it all is from the gentle dreamworld of Stephen Foster's plantations with their slaves mourning the good master in the cold, cold ground.

Listen to the Mocking Bird

Septimus Winner, the 27-year-old Philadelphia shopkeeper and music teacher, had been composing songs for only about a year when he produced "Listen to the Mocking Bird" in 1854. Apparently the song did not sell especially well after Winner published it the next year, for he sold the copyright shortly for $5.00 to Lee & Walker, another Philadelphia publisher. He most surely regretted this hasty move; the song became immensely famous in this country and abroad, was a favorite of Lincoln, and purportedly sold millions of copies in sheet music over the following five decades. As with "Whispering Hope" and many other of his songs, "Mocking Bird" was released under the pseudonym Alice Hawthorne (a little tribute to his mother, Mary Ann Hawthorne Winner). Other than Hawthorne and his own name, he also published under the names Percy Guyer, Mark Mason and Apsley Street. It was an era passionate for the *nom de plume.*

Charles Claghorn, in his slim biography of the composer (see Bibliography), supplies a bit of information on Richard Milburn, the co-author of *Mocking Bird*:

> There are many stories regarding the origin of the song, but Mr. Winner reiterated that the melody came to him through the whistling of a colored boy, named Dick, who ran errands for the store. Dick Milburn, who was known as "Whistling Dick," had been a beggar, collecting pennies, nickels and dimes from persons on the streets of Philadelphia, while he whistled and played upon his guitar. At various times he imitated the warble of the mocking bird. . . . It was with this inspiration that he composed his famous piece, while the colored boy was given a job in the store.

As can be seen from the cover of the rare first edition reproduced in this collection, Winner gave Milburn a prominent credit line as composer of the melody. None of the subsequent editions, however, mentions Milburn's contribution. In any case, the song fashioned by the Philadelphia whistler and the pseudonymous shopkeeper has retained a freshness and charm well after its centenary has passed.

The Little Brown Jug

Like his older brother Septimus, Joseph Eastburn Winner (1837–1918) favored a pseudonym for his work as songwriter and chose to use his middle name alone as his signature. Joseph's "Eastburn" was far less prolific that Septimus' "Alice Hawthorne," producing only twenty-odd pieces during a period of approximately thirty years. But Joseph's career was quite like his brother's in that he also operated a music store in his native Philadelphia (beginning in 1854) and published music under his own imprint (beginning in the late 1860s). In fact, the two were apparently friendly rivals in almost all their pursuits. As Eastburn, Joseph composed Civil War songs, ballads, a few piano pieces, and comic songs—his most characteristic and successful genre. Among the latter are "Oil on the Brain" (1865), "The Yankees Boast That They Can Make Clocks," "When Mother Married Pap" (1868), "The Kettle and the Clock," "That's Where the Laugh Comes In" (1893) and—his only big popular hit— "The Little Brown Jug" (1869).

It is possible that the idea for "The Little Brown Jug" was not original with Winner; there exists another song of the same title bearing an 1868 copyright notice (by Oliver Ditson) with an almost identical cover design; but the music of this song, by one W. F. Wellman, Jr., is totally different from Winner's, as is the rather overly elaborate text by the ever-busy George Cooper. In any case, this is really of small concern, for it is Winner's "Little Brown Jug" that swept to popularity and survives because of its memorable, ingenuous tune and its disarmingly direct text. When the song was a new best seller, the advocates of the Temperance Movement must have gone into frenzies over its bluntly stated, respectability-be-damned idea of pleasure.

Joseph Winner, as publisher, frequently brought out pieces by Eastburn, the composer. He must have taken some delight in promoting Eastburn's works; his ad copy for Eastburn's "Matchless Schottische" reads: "Universally admired; the time well marked, the melody lovely; one of those enchanting little pieces that we can't KEEP STILL while listening to, and which, after hearing, we find ourselves unconsciously humming." His copy for "The Little Brown Jug" was more to the point: "One of the most popular Comic Songs in existence."

Long, Long Ago

For some reason this graceful English piece of the 1830s apparently has come to be regarded as a children's song. It is not. As a reading of it will verify, it is a love song, one touched with wistfulness and uncertainty: a lover of long ago has returned to renew old ties, but have old feelings really been retained? We never find out. The singer remains doubtful though wanting desperately to believe.

The song is the work of Thomas Haynes Bayly (1797–1839), gentleman poet, songwriter and dramatist. Bayly pursued all of these activities for a livelihood and was considered a rather talented hack. He produced some of the more elegant song hits of his day, including "I'd Be a Butterfly," "She Wore a Wreath of Roses" and "The Soldier's Tear." A prestigious British song anthology of the 1890s (the four-volume *British Minstrelsie*) remembered Bayly not unkindly as

> a master in his peculiar line—that of sentimental song. He was the forerunner of the composers of that whole series of namby-pamby stuff which has an enormous run at the present day. But his compositions were superior to what has followed; and some of his best songs, words and music, will not die, when all the later stuff has perished.

"Long, Long Ago" was chosen for the British anthology as representative of Bayly's best work. The song was as popular in America almost as long as it was in England. It was published in New York within a few years of its first appearance in London.

Lorena

"Lorena" is surely one of the most attractive songs to emerge from mid-nineteenth-century America. It was enormously popular during the Civil War era and beyond and survives in numerous arrangements. It has been used frequently in films, especially westerns; Max Steiner's use of the song in his score for John Ford's *The Searchers* (1956) was particularly effective. It is also the subject of a charming and authoritative book entitled *The Sweetheart of the Civil War. The True Story of the Song "Lorena"* (see Bibliography under Emurian). "Lorena" was the work of two interesting nineteenth-century figures who shared the same name but who were not related: Rev. Henry DeLafayette Webster (1824–1896), author of the poem, and Joseph Philbrick Webster (1819–1875), the composer. The author was an itinerant minister with the Universalist Church who traveled mostly in Ohio, Indiana, Wisconsin and Illinois. The composer, born in New Hampshire, was also a traveler; he lived at various times in Boston, New York and parts of the South and Midwest; his last home was in Wisconsin. The paths of the two Websters crossed in Madison, Indiana, in 1856; they became friends and together produced "Lorena," which was published in Chicago in 1857. The two men and their families soon moved on again in different directions, but their paths crossed once more in Wisconsin in the early 1860s. Here they collaborated for the second and last time on a sequel to their hit "Lorena" entitled "Paul Vane, or Lorena's Reply" (1863), which did not duplicate the success of the original.

The little scenario outlined in the verses of "Lorena" was based on a detailed romantic episode from the author's earlier years. The name of the real girl from the minister's past provides the key to the etymology of the fictitious name Lorena: she was Martha Ellen Blocksom (called Ella). Webster initially used the name Bertha for her in his poem, but it did not fit the musical syllables the composer wanted; so he took components from the girl's real name, combined them appropriately with Edgar Allan Poe's "lost Lenore," and created Lorena, a name not in existence before the song.

Marching Through Georgia

"Kingdom Coming" (1862), which celebrated the Day of Jubilee at hand, was Henry Clay Work's first war song; "Marching Through Georgia" (1865), which celebrated the Jubilee that had now occurred, was his last. (He subsequently turned his attentions to such postwar efforts as "Lillie of the Snowstorm, or Please, Father, Let Us In!") "Georgia" maintained its popularity far beyond the war years, however, and this was partly due to Work's device of framing the historical event as a kind of flashback. George F. Root took note of this fact in his 1891 autobiography:

> "Marching Thro' Georgia" is more played and sung at the present time than any other song of the war. This is not only on account of the intrinsic merit of its words and music, but because it is *retrospective*. Other war songs, "The Battle-Cry of Freedom" for example, were for exciting the patriotic feeling on *going in* to the war or the battle; "Marching Thro' Georgia" is a glorious remembrance on coming triumphantly out, and so has been more appropriate to soldiers' and other gatherings ever since.

The event which the song celebrates is of course, "Maj. Gen. Sherman's Famous March 'from Atlanta to the Sea,'" as the cover announces. Like any good propaganda piece, the song takes no notice of the actual realities of the situation it glorifies. The fact that Sherman's devastating month-long march at the end of 1864, so filled with senseless destruction, came after the Confederacy was already substantially defeated and that it was motivated more by imperious self-aggrandizement than by military necessity—these facts could not concern Henry Clay Work in his role of commercial glorifier of the cause. The song is in considerable contrast to "Kingdom Coming" with its naturalism (one-sided, to be sure) and satire. In "Marching Through Georgia," Work casts a kind of romantic haze over the affair: the marauding Union soldiers are seen as "Sherman's dashing Yankee boys"; the desperate Georgians are merely "saucy rebels"; the pillaging of food is coyly dismissed with "How the turkeys gobbled which our commissary found!" All of this is seen at a distance as a "glorious remembrance" by the veterans pictured in the first verse as they trot out the old bugle and congratulate themselves for carrying "the flag that makes you free!"

Maryland, My Maryland!

This was one of the most popular rallying songs in the Confederacy during the Civil War, rivalling "Dixie" as "the song of the Southern people." The words were written by the Baltimore poet James Ryder Randall (1839–1908) in April 1861 at Poydras College near New Roads, Louisiana. He read in the *New Orleans Delta* the account of Massachusetts troops being fired upon as they passed through Baltimore; one of Randall's friends was the first casualty when the Union soldiers returned fire. "I had long been absent from my native city," the poet later recounted, "and the startling event there inflamed my mind. That night I could not sleep. . . . I proceeded to write the song of 'My Maryland.' . . . The whole poem of nine stanzas as originally written, was dashed off rapidly, when once begun."

The tune of "Maryland, My Maryland!" is that of a German folksong first published in 1799. It is also well known in its use with two other poems, the German carol "O Tannenbaum" and the college song "Lauriger Horatius." Jennie Cary, member of a prominent Confederate-activist family in Baltimore, conceived the idea of using the old tune with Randall's poem shortly after it appeared in the Baltimore press. Miss Cary also introduced the song to a mass audience under dramatic circumstances. She was one in a small party permitted to visit General P. G. T. Beauregard near Fairfax County Court House, Virginia, in July 1861 shortly after the first battle of Manassas. In darkness she stood before a tent and performed the stirring song for Beauregard's troops, who gradually joined in the refrain.

The musical setting was first published by the Baltimore firm Miller & Beacham in October 1861. The first edition carries no attribution of authorship, only stating that it was "Written by A Baltimorean in Louisianna." The musical adaptation is credited to an anonymous "C. E." (probably Charles Ellerbrock, a soldier-composer whose name appears in later editions as arranger). Randall does receive credit in the first Confederate edition published in January 1862 by A. E. Blackmar & Bro., a leading New Orleans firm that subsequently brought out other songs by Randall. This edition also carries the credit "Music by a Lady of Baltimore," apparently referring to Jennie Cary.

My Old Kentucky Home

Stephen Foster composed this song probably in 1852 and it was published in January 1853. There are several legends that connect the piece to Federal Hill, the summer home of Judge John Rowan in Bardstown, Kentucky, but there is no documentary evidence from the period to prove that Foster had much connection with the place. Judge Rowan, at one time United States Senator from Kentucky, was a cousin of Stephen's father and well known to the Foster family. Stephen probably visited Federal Hill in the 1840s, but it is most unlikely that he composed "My Old Kentucky Home" there or that he even had the house in mind when he composed it.

Foster's manuscript workbook reveals that the original title of the poem was "Poor Uncle Tom, Good Night" and that the text varied from that of the final published version. Each verse originally ended with the line "Den poor Uncle Tom, good night." Foster was perhaps inspired by Harriet Beecher Stowe's recently published *Uncle Tom's Cabin* (1851) or attempting to capitalize on the book's new fame. In any case, legends die hard, and Federal Hill is still secure in Foster lore and is a museum and tourist attraction. Kentucky took the song as its own long ago and finally proclaimed it the official state song in 1928.

The Ocean Burial

Themes of death and dying were among the most prominent in popular Victorian literature, especially in the ballads. These themes were particularly attractive when worked within the great tradition of the home song, for if it was sufficient to celebrate the joys of home simply by enumerating them ("Home on the Range," "Old Folks at Home"), how much more poignant to have those joys reflected upon by a wandering youth as death overtakes him. George N. Allen's "The Ocean Burial," published by Ditson in 1850 (in its original printing an elaborate "Song & Quartette") is a prime example of the genre. Here, for six long verses, a youth on a ship at sea lies dying (of homesickness or seasickness?—"He had wasted and pined 'till o'er his brow, The death-shade had slowly passed"). He ruminates on his home, parents, sister and his desire to be buried in the family grave. At thought of the sweetheart, his reverie reaches a climax of grotesque pathos:

> In the hair she hath wreathed, shall the sea snake hiss!
> And the brow she hath pressed, shall the cold wave kiss!

In the last verse, just as the ship nears home (a twist of the knife), he dies and, despite his prior directions to the contrary, is lowered over the side by his shipmates: "They have buried him there, in the deep, deep sea."

The original text of the ballad, by the Reverend Edwin H. Chapin, was published in the *Southern Literary Messenger* in 1839. Sometime later (probably in the 1870s), after Allen's setting had traveled west, an anonymous poet altered the text, giving it relevance to life on the frontier. A cowboy replaces the young sailor, and he sings: "Oh bury me not on the lone prairie." It is in this version, of course, that "The Ocean Burial" has survived so handily to the present day.

Oh, Dem Golden Slippers!

One distinctive quality that marked the livelier minstrel songs of James A. Bland was a certain religious fervor. It is evident in "Oh, Dem Golden Slippers!" (copyrighted 1879), which sings of preparations for the judgment day when the faithful will "walk de golden street." The use of religious subject matter was a departure from earlier minstrel songs such as Work's "Kingdom Coming," in which the concept of jubilee was used as a metaphor for the emancipation from slavery. Its music, too, has the spirit of a gospel song, though it also carries suggestions of the cakewalk and ragtime that would soon emerge and flower.

"Golden Slippers" is from the earlier phase of Bland's career as professional songwriter and minstrel performer during which he composed his most famous pieces. It was a career that spanned about 25 years, roughly from the mid-1870s to the end of the century. At his death in 1911 he was apparently an obscure figure; there were no memorials, no obituaries.

The restoration of his name began in the late 1930s with the publication of an article by Kelly Miller (see Bibliography), a professor at Howard University, who pieced together bits of information on Bland's life with the help of a few surviving relatives. In 1940 Bland's "Carry Me Back to Old Virginny" was adopted as the official state song of

Virginia. The first collection of his songs was published in 1946 as edited by the folk-music scholar Charles Haywood, who also provided an excellent commentary on the composer. Also in that year a stone was placed at his grave (which had been located by Kelly Miller during his research) in Merion Cemetery in Bala-Cynwyd, Pennsylvania, a suburb of Philadelphia; this memorial was sponsored by the Lyons Clubs of Virginia. Completing this first wave of new recognition was the appearance of a fictionalized but useful biography of the composer in 1951.

Oh My Darling Clementine

This was not a song of the Gold Rush period despite the fact that is is about the daughter of a miner, "A Forty-niner." Curiously, the text first appeared in an obscure 1863 song entitled "Down By the River Lived a Maiden" by the prolific songwriter H. S. Thompson and published by Oliver Ditson of Boston. Twenty-one years later, Ditson again published the text, but this time with the subsequently familiar tune, as "Oh My Darling Clementine," words and music credited to one Percy Montrose. No documentation seems to exist that might solve this little puzzle of authorship.

In any case, when darling Clementine made her first appearance it was in a song that surely was not intended as comic: "Down By the River Lived a Maiden" was a song about the daughter of a prospector who has an accident one morning while tending her ducks and falls into a river; her boy friend is at the scene but he cannot swim so he watches helplessly as the girl drowns. (H. S. Thompson must have been in a predominantly grim mood during the war years of 1863: two of his other titles that year were "Keep This Bible Near Your Heart" and "I'm Lonely Since My Mother Died." He had first scored a decade earlier with "Lily Dale," 1852: ". . . the death damp was on the pure white brow Of my poor lost Lily Dale.") Somehow, in the 21 years between 1863 and 1884, the tale of poor Clementine—"lost and gone forever"—came to be regarded as a suitable text for a rollicking comedy piece. It was included in collections of college songs immediately after its publication and became the vehicle for countless spoofs and parodies.

Oh! Susanna

Foster's "Oh! Susanna" was first performed in public on 11 September 1847 in Pittsburgh. The setting of the modest premiere (it was sung by a local quintette) was Andrews' Eagle Ice Cream Saloon, undoubtedly a proper home for "Susanna's" zany contradictions and farce-comedy. Foster is said to have written the song for informal use by a men's social group of which he and his brother Morrison were members. Within fourteen months of "Susanna's" first public hearing, at least eight different copyright claims for the piece were registered by publishers in New York, Massachusetts and Maryland. Foster's name appeared as composer on a few of these unauthorized versions but he received no remuneration whatsoever for them. This situation, however, was largely brought on by the youthful and inexperienced composer himself. He apparently handed out numerous manuscript copies of his early songs to any performer who would accept them. Some of the copies passed into the hands of publishers eager for potential new hits "As Sung By the Christy Minstrels" or some other famous troupe. In this case, the song was widely known even before it came from the presses.

If Foster ever received any money for "Oh! Susanna" it probably came from William C. Peters, a music dealer and publisher in Cincinnati who had published four of Foster's earliest songs. In an article written three years after Foster's death, Robert Peebles Nevin (a friend of the composer) stated that Peters asked for both "Susanna" and "Uncle Ned" and that Foster gave them to him without thought of receiving payment. Peters published both songs in 1848 and, according to Nevin, gave the composer nothing for "Uncle Ned" and one hundred dollars for "Susanna."

Of all Foster's dialect songs, "Susanna" seems closest to being an authentic folk piece. Musically it has the snap and dash typical of so many regional banjo and fiddle tunes; textually it has the heady nonsense of an Elizabethan ballad transformed by the rowdy American frontier. Certainly the thousands of adventurers and homesteaders who immediately took "Susanna" with them to the West, eager for gold and land, made her their very own.

Old Black Joe

Foster composed this song probably a short time before he moved permanently from Pittsburgh to New York in the late summer or early fall of 1860. It is perhaps difficult today to be in company with "Old Black Joe" and not feel some embarrassment. "Gone are the days" when it might have been possible to take the song at something like face value, without a century of social change to weigh heavily on its naïve "plantation" clichés. If one can take it on its own terms, however, and especially within the context of the last four years of Foster's career, "Old Black Joe" can be judged a superior achievement. It has a directness of expression and a grace and naturalness of melodic line that place it near "Old Folks at Home" and his other finest ballads. The text is in Foster's own poetic language with no trace of dialect (he had not written expressly for the minstrel stage for about seven years). There may be more than a little of Foster himself injected into the song: with his mother, father and various other members of his family dead, with his marriage on shaky ground and his finances unstable, he could well have longed for former times when his "heart was young and gay" and could almost have heard the "gentle voices calling."

Old Dan Tucker

Reprinted here with its elaborately illustrated title page is the first edition of this famous old minstrel piece as published by Charles H. Keith of Boston in 1843. It is one of *Old Dan Emmit's* [*sic*] *Original Banjo Melodies*, a series of seven pieces issued that year by the publisher. Though the text of "Old Dan Tucker" was indeed written by Emmett, the melody was not his composition. Its origin is not known (Nathan, p. 301; see Bibliography). It is altogether appropriate that the first edition of the piece should have originated in Boston, for it was here in March 1843 that Emmett (violin and banjo), Frank Brower (bones), William Whitlock (banjo) and Richard Pelham (tambourine) gave their first full-evening performance as the Virginia Minstrels: the first minstrel show. The program was a mixture of songs ("Old Dan Tucker," among others) sung by one or more of the group accompanied by the instruments, skits, jokes, dancing and bits of solo instrumental work. Within a matter of weeks they gained a tremendous reputation and set off on a tour of England. Though the Virginia Minstrels would disperse in about a year and a half, they had pioneered a form of entertainment—of black-face minstrels banding together to form a whole show—that dominated the American popular theater for decades.

Old Folks at Home

Composed in Pittsburgh and published in New York in October 1851, this was undoubtedly Foster's most popular song and the one that earned him (and later his widow and daughter) the largest royalties from sheet-music sales. It is the song that is perhaps most immediately associated with the composer's name. A long-noted irony in this respect is that Foster's name did not appear during his lifetime on the published song, as can be seen from the cover of the first edition reproduced in this collection. (His name did appear as composer after the copyright of the song was renewed in 1879.) It was of course Edwin P. Christy who was credited as having "written and composed" "Old Folks at Home," and Foster himself was responsible for this. He apparently sold to Christy the right to be publicized as composer of the song for the sum of $5.00. Eight months after "Old Folks" appeared, Foster regretted his action and tried unsuccessfully to nullify the agreement.

The plantation scene of Foster's celebration of the good life among the old folks was originally set on the Pedee River. Drafts of the poem in his manuscript workbook read:

Way down upon de Pedee ribber
Far far away

and then:

Swanee
Way down upon de ~~Pedee~~ ribber
Far far away.

He perhaps decided to use the two-syllable corruption of Florida's Suwannee because the initial vowel is more graceful for singing. It is difficult to imagine what subsequent generations of Tin Pan Alley lyricists would have done without the corrupt but musical Swanee to fall back on. The word eventually served almost as well as the mythical Dixie to conjure a stereotyped Southern setting.

The Old Oaken Bucket

In the New York newspaper the *Republican Chronicle*, there appeared in the issue of June 3, 1818, a deathless bit of American verse with the crushingly prosaic title, "The Bucket." This rustic effusion had been written the preceding year by Samuel Woodworth (1785–1842) of Massachusetts, at the time editor of the *Chronicle* and celebrated as author of a curious historical novel. Woodworth's subsequently famous bucket that hung in the old family well absolutely pales in comparison with the subsequently forgotten novel: an ambitious two-volume affair entitled *The Champions of Freedom* (1816) that was, in the words of *The Oxford Companion to American Literature*, "a fantastic moral romance with the War of 1812 as background to a plot involving the spirit of George Washington as a 'Mysterious Chief' who guides the destinies of Decatur, Harrison, Jackson, and other heroes of the time." (Ah, what a caprice of the historical muse to keep the homely "Bucket" swinging and wash the weighty *Champions* down the drain of oblivion!) The novel was not Woodworth's only effort in the larger forms—he also wrote plays—but, perhaps wisely, "verse-making and love-making claimed most of his time" (Dressler, p. 231; see Bibliography). He also worked fitfully at being a printer, journalist and wanderer (especially when various business schemes collapsed).

"The Bucket" was reprinted in several journals and eventually received at least three different musical settings, in which it came to be known as "The Old Oaken Bucket." One very popular version, published around 1834, used a Scotch melody by Robert Smith (from the older song "Jesse, the Flower of Dumblaine"). The version that became the familiar standard first appeared around 1850 and used another borrowed tune, that of the song "Araby's Daughter." The original "Araby's Daughter," by George Kiallmark (1781–1835), an English composer and violinist, had considerable popularity on its own. It was a setting of a text from Thomas Moore's *Lalla Rookh* (1817), a group of four Oriental tales in verse with a connecting prose narrative, and was published in several American editions in the 1820s.

Old Rosin the Beau

The folksong authority James F. Leisy states in his excellent book *The Folk Song Abecedary* (see Bibliography) that the tune of this very old comic song originated as an Irish folk melody to a patriotic text entitled "Men of the West." He says that it was introduced in America with the anonymous "Old Rosin" text in 1838, the year the Osbourn edition reprinted here was published in Philadelphia. Other early American printings call "Old Rosin" "a favorite Southern ballad," and it is known to have become a popular drinking song on the frontier, especially during the gold-rush days. The members of the Falcon Club rowing team, pictured by Osbourn in their scull on the Schuylkill River, were perhaps also fond of drinking songs; he dedicates this one to them "with much respect."

Among the early sheet-music editions there are wide differences in text and tune, but the first verse as published by Atwill (New York) became the more-or-less standard version:

> I live for the good of the nation,
> My sons are all growing low,
> I hope that my next generation,
> Will resemble Old Rosin the beau,
> I've travell'd this country all over,
> And now to the next I will go,
> I know that good quarters await me,
> To welcome Old Rosin the beau.

All the early versions agree, however, on the major features: Old Rosin likes to drink, and he is dying. As in so many folk or quasi-folk pieces, death is treated in an offhand and casual manner:

> Get four or five jovial young fellows
> And let them all staggering go
> And dig a deep hole in the meadow
> And in it toss Rosin the beau.

Decades after the song was first published in America, and the gold rush was a fading memory, "Old Rosin the Beau" furnished the melody for a song that became associated with the state of Washington when it entered the union in 1889. It was Francis D. Henry's well-known "Acres of Clams," which celebrated farming in the Northwest over prospecting:

> I've wandered all over this country
> Prospecting and digging for gold . . .
>
> For one who got rich by mining
> I saw there were hundreds grew poor . . .
>
> I rolled up my grub in my blanket,
> I left all my tools on the ground,
> I started one morning to shank it
> For the country they call Puget Sound . . .
>
> No longer the slave of ambition,
> I laugh at the world and its shams,
> And think of my happy condition
> Surrounded by acres of clams . . . .

Pop Goes the Weasel

Not a great deal seems to be known about the origins of this famous song. Published editions first appeared in England and America in the same year, 1853. According to James Fuld (see Bibliography), the English edition had no text and identified the piece as an old English dance. The first American edition, by Berry & Gordon (immediate predecessor of S. T. Gordon, publisher of the similar 1859 edition reprinted here), did have the text but in a version no longer totally familiar. As can be seen from the 1859 printing, the text is a curious mixture of comedy verses in dialect (indicating that the piece was used on the minstrel stage), passages satirizing English social and political attitudes ("John Bull tells . . . How Uncle Sam used *Uncle Tom*, While he makes some white folks *slaves* at home . . ."), directions for dancing ("form two lines as straight as a string") and finally, topical references to the temperance movement and the World's Fair. This strange conglomerate is clearly an American invention. More familiar versions, which include the phrase "All around the mulberry bush, the monkey chased the weasel," apparently did not appear until the twentieth century.

Reuben and Rachel

This most charming duet apparently made its first appearance in Boston in 1871 as published by White, Smith & Perry. No special facts about the song seem to have been recorded, nor have either Harry Birch, the author, or William Gooch, the composer, found a place in the reference books. This is surprising, for the piece is one of delicate craftsmanship and shows the hand of seasoned professionals; one might have imagined the authors to be prominent in their field. The song's most unusual feature is the use of the sixteen-bar introduction in C minor—a passage, and a key, heard only once—to begin a song that will be in the key of E-flat Major. (Is it this curious introduction that alone gives the piece a slightly exotic, perhaps Near Eastern, touch?) The simple four-bar bridge between introduction and verse marked "Till ready to sing" is an early appearance of what would become decades later Tin Pan Alley's indispensable "Vamp till ready." (Incidentally, the vamp should be used only between verses and not at the very end of the piece; close at the light double bar in the middle of the last line of music.) On the cover we see an engraving of the couple facing each other, Reuben in his broad-brimmed hat and long overcoat and Rachel in her bonnet and shawl. His left foot goes forward, her right foot goes backward; their hands are outstretched, in motion: they are dancing their courtship.

Rock'd in the Cradle of the Deep

Here we have one of the great favorites of parlor recitalists and church soloists for perhaps the better part of a century, especially contraltos and basses, who have such fun with the last line descending literally into the depths. (In 1975 the 135-year-old song was available in different arrangements as trombone and tuba solos with band.) The poem is by an American, Mrs. Emma Hart Willard, a resident of Troy, New York, who reportedly wrote it during a voyage from Europe to America in 1832. *British Minstrelsie* (see Bibliography) reports Mrs. Willard's dates as 1787–1870. She ran a school in Troy and during the year 1839 her music instructor was the young Englishman Joseph Philip Knight (1812–1887), already an established songwriter. During his year in America, he composed a musical setting for Mrs. Willard's 1832 poem of faith on the high seas; it was published promptly by C. E. Horn of New York in 1840. Knight returned to England and in later years became a minister of the Church of England.

The words and music of "Rock'd in the Cradle of the Deep" present an attractive unity. The tune is good, if repetitive, and the accompaniment discreet; Knight's repeated trills give a little color and perhaps a suggestion of ocean breezes, especially the long trill over the singer's final phrase. Particularly felicitous is Mrs. Willard's central metaphor of the ocean as a great cradle. One can perhaps readily understand how she came upon the idea if one visualizes the poet in her bunk bed at night on that sailing ship crossing the Atlantic in 1832.

Shew! Fly, Don't Bother Me

Sigmund Spaeth, in *Read 'Em and Weep*, his amusing book about old songs, calls "Shew! Fly" the most popular nonsense song of the Civil War (the statement is not corroborated, however, in the literature on Civil War music). If the song was popular during the war, it circulated only in oral tradition; there was apparently no published version until White, Smith & Perry of Boston brought one out in 1869 (the edition reprinted here). Spaeth credits the text to Billy Reeves and the music to Frank Campbell, as do several of the early editions.

There have been other claims of authorship, however. An edition was published in New York, also in 1869, as "Composed by T. Brigham Bishop" and proclaimed to be the "Original copy and only authorized edition." It was published by Bishop himself and identified as a " 'Walk Round' From the negro [*sic*] farce the 'Cook.' " An interesting clipping in the Song Index at The New York Public Library's Music Division substantiates Bishop's claim. The clipping —a leter from Charles E. Sturges to the *New York Herald Tribune* of February 26, 1926—quotes one Herbert Renton as stating that Bishop, a songwriter who was in charge of a company of Negro soldiers during the Civil War, heard some of his men using expressions such as "I'se feelin' like a mornin' star" and "Go 'way coon; shoo, fly, don't bother me" and strung them together to form the text. The letter-writer Sturges goes on to say: "I was in position to know something about 'Shoo Fly,' as Rollin Howard, who arranged and had printed the only published edition of the song, was my stage partner in 1869, the year it was published by a Boston music firm. I remember very distinctly we did not know who was the author. [On the first page of music of the copy reprinted here, the words are credited to Billy Reeves.] Rollin Howard's name appeared on the title page, but he did not claim to be the author; his rights to the song were not disputed. . . . 'Shoo Fly' at that time was sung and danced in every minstrel company and variety show by the leading song-and-dance men. It had a very long run at Bryant's Minstrels on Fourteenth Street in the latter part of 1869 and early part of 1870, sung and danced by Dan Bryant and Dave Reed as a duet."

T. Brigham Bishop was associated with the minstrel team of Delehanty and Hengler in the late 1860s and was known for such popular pieces as "Kittie Wells" (1861), "Leaf By Leaf the Roses Fall" (1865) and "When We Marched to the Roll of the Drum" (1866).

Silver Threads Among the Gold

It must be conceded that the name Eben Eugene Rexford is not among the more prominent in nineteenth-century American letters. Yet there are two public memorials to him, one in Shiocton, Wisconsin, where he lived most of his life, and the other near Johnsburg, New York; the latter is a plaque that reads: "In Memory of Eben Eugene Rexford, Author of the famous ballad 'Silver Threads Among the Gold.' Born at this Place July 16, 1847 [*sic*]. Died October 15, 1916." He was born there in 1848 and taken as a child to Wisconsin. There he conducted his several careers as local postmaster, editor of a farm journal and author of light verse and several books on horticulture, including *Home Floriculture* and *Grandmother's Garden.* In 1872 Connecticut-born Hart Pease Danks (1834–1903), a carpenter, singer, choir leader and songwriter, read one of Rexford's verses in the farm journal and wrote to him offering to buy it for use as a song text. Rexford, probably unused to such response to his work, reportedly sent Danks a whole sheaf of poems. Among them was "Silver Threads Among the Gold," surely a poem to turn the head of any aspiring Victorian songwriter: it caught so perfectly a certain contemporary spirit and was so invitingly exploitable as lyric commerce in the middle-class parlor trade. The song was published in 1873 and did a flourishing business. The fashionable message of the song—that romantic love remains always young even though bodies age and wrinkle—was apparently lost on Danks's wife; she left the forty-year-old composer the year after "Silver Threads" appeared.

Danks made at least two attempts to break into show business, but though he had the collaboration of writers of greater renown and experience than Eben Rexford, he failed to secure the success he had enjoyed with the Wisconsin farm journalist. With the popular lyricist George Cooper (see notes on "Sweet Genevieve") he wrote *Pauline; or The Belle of Saratoga* (1873), an operetta that strained for worldly sophistication, and with Fanny Crosby (1820–1915), the celebrated blind poetess and hymn writer, he produced *Zanie* (1887), a Gypsy spectacle set in the English countryside. Both works were published but there is no record that either received a New York production. Danks also collaborated on a school operetta with Miss Crosby, *Conquered by Kindness* (1881), that fared better than his more ambitious stage pieces.

Sweet By and By

It may be that the venerable old Gospel number "Sweet By and By" is the only famous song written in a drugstore; it is *certainly* the only famous song written in a drugstore in Elkhorn, Wisconsin. This was the town that the composer Joseph Philbrick Webster settled in with his family in 1859. As teacher, performer (he played a Stradivarius violin) and especially as composer of the celebrated song "Lorena" (1857), Webster became the reigning musical celebrity of Elkhorn and remained so until his death there in 1875. Prior to Elkhorn, Webster had wandered for years as a somewhat eccentric musical jack-of-all-trades. He started his career as a kind of musical prodigy in rural New Hampshire, studied music for three years in Boston, toured for six years as a singer, composed numerous successful songs and traveled in the South and Midwest as a piano salesman and teacher. He named his three sons Joseph Haydn Webster, Louis Beethoven Webster and Frederick Handel Webster.

One day in 1867, so the story goes, Webster strolled into the Elkhorn drugstore owned by his friend Sanford Fillmore Bennett (1836–1898), who wrote verse on the side. Webster was in a gloomy mood and, ostensibly to cheer him up, Bennett scribbled down some verses that dealt with the joys awaiting the Christian on the other side of the grave. Whether or not this did the trick is not recorded; in any case, Webster proceeded to set the druggist's verses and "Sweet By and By" was on its way. It was published the next year in *The Signet Ring,* a collection of Gospel songs that included other pieces by the two men. On Webster's gravestone in Elkhorn's Hazel Ridge Cemetery are inscribed the words "Composer, Patriot, Student, Genius" as well as the opening bars of music of "Sweet By and By."

Far removed from this site, the song reached something like its apotheosis in 1915 in the hands of Charles Ives (1874–1954); he used it with great effect in his *Second Orchestral Set* as the basis of the stirring final movement that recaptures in music the composer's experience on a New York subway platform on the day the *Lusitania* went down. Joseph Webster and Sanford Bennett would have been amazed.

Sweet Genevieve

The poet and lyricist George Cooper (1840–1927) was in his early twenties when he met Stephen Foster in New York at the beginning of the 1860s. He served briefly in the Civil War in the Twenty-second New York Infantry and returned to collaborate with Foster on some twenty-three songs, many of them comic ("If You've Only Got a Moustache," 1862) or based on Civil War themes ("Willie Has Gone to the War," 1863). Cooper was one of the composer's closest friends of his last years, identified his body in the morgue of Bellevue Hospital and sent a telegram to Stephen's brother Morrison. With his collaboration with Foster serving as a kind of apprenticeship, Cooper went on to become a thoroughly seasoned and prolific writer of commercial song texts, apparently earning a living solely by this activity. His obituary in *The New York Times* of September 28, 1927, states that he had written over two hundred songs.

His single most popular piece was the nostalgic "Sweet Genevieve" (1869) with music by another veteran of the popular-music business, Henry Tucker. The inevitable "human interest" story connected with the song, as reported by James J. Geller (see Bibliography) and others, is that Genevieve was the real-life bride of Cooper who died shortly after their marriage. Geller's version of the story has it that Cooper wrote the poem "fifteen years after his sacred loss," which is unlikely because (supposing the poem was written in 1869) it would make Cooper a bridegroom at age fourteen. John Tasker Howard states in *Our American Music* that the sacred loss occurred in 1869, which is more plausible. Though Cooper's text promises the dead girl that "My heart shall never, never rove: Thou art my only guiding star," he made another apparently good marriage and produced three children who survived him.

Unlike the reputed heroine of the song, "Sweet Genevieve" lived a long and useful life. When the initial copyright expired in 1897, it was renewed for another 28-year period by the heirs of Henry Tucker and reissued by William A. Pond, the original publisher. Furthermore, the company put out ten different arrangements and transcriptions of "Genevieve," as listed on the cover of the 1897 edition; Pond was going all out to make as much money as possible on the old favorite while the copyright lasted. Cooper's obituary states that the song "enjoyed a return to popularity" as late as 1925 and that "its revival brought Cooper more money in royalties than he received from the song when it appeared [originally]." If Cooper did make money on "Genevieve" during the last two years of his life, it was probably through the generosity of the American Society of Composers, Authors and Publishers, of which he was an honorary member. Cooper had no legal rights in the song, for he apparently sold the poem outright to Henry Tucker in 1869 for five dollars.

Tenting on the Old Camp Ground

Until the great success of this song brought him a fairly substantial income, its composer earned a modest living largely as an itinerant singer traveling about New England in a wagon, giving concerts by himself in country towns. Walter Kittredge (born in 1834 in New Hampshire) composed the song on his violin apparently during the evening before he was to be drafted into the Union Army in 1863. He was rejected, however, because of a recent bout with rheumatic fever, but the song inspired by the impending induction did go to the front and became a melancholy favorite with troops on both sides as the war dragged on to its last days.

Not surprisingly, Kittredge's gentle, sad reverie on the long night of war and the reluctant "dawn of peace" was at first rejected by a Boston publisher, who was probably looking for another good patriotic rabble-rouser like Root's "Battle Cry of Freedom." The song did not see print until it was performed and championed as an anti-war piece by the famous singing Hutchinson Family—always alert to a new cause—and Asa Hutchinson, a founding member of the group, used his personal influence with the Oliver Ditson Company, which had made a lot of money from other songs of the family. For his services as agent, Asa shared royalties equally with Kittredge, thus proving that virtue is not always solely its own reward.

Ditson published the song in 1864 as arranged by M. F. H. Smith, and if it was his idea to use the Reveille bugle call, unaccompanied, and a four-measure variation on it to introduce the song, he was indeed a clever and sensitive arranger. The sentiments expressed in "Tenting" were sufficiently universal to keep it in currency years beyond the specific events that inspired it. During the 1960s it was used as a protest song by Pete Seeger and others who opposed the war in Viet Nam and it was published, without a word of the original changed, in *Songs for Peace* (1966), compiled by the Student Peace Union.

There Is a Tavern in the Town

A case has been made for the possibility that this originated as a traditional miners' song in Cornwall, England, but it became famous as an American college song published in the 1880s. It first appeared in William H. Hills' *Students' Songs* (1883 edition), the popular and influential series that also introduced "My Bonnie." It was subsequently anthologized widely and published in separate sheet-music editions such as the one of 1891 reprinted here.

"There Is a Tavern in the Town," along with "A Hot Time in the Old Town" (1896), is among the best known nineteenth-century "male" songs associated with drinking and carousing; it might be noted, however, that it was apparently written from a female point of view ("my dear love sits him down," "He left me," etc.).

Tramp! Tramp! Tramp! (or The Prisoner's Hope)

In the same year that George F. Root brought out his "Just Before the Battle, Mother" he produced this second big war hit. Within six months after its appearance in January 1864 it had sold 100,000 copies in sheet music, according to the publisher Root & Cady. It was composed for the "extra" New Year's number of the company's house organ *The Song Messenger of the Northwest*, and Root described the circumstances in his autobiography:

> One day my brother said, "We must have that song or we can not get the paper into the hands of the people by New Year's Day; go write it now while it is on your mind." In two hours I brought him the song. We tried it over and he said: "I must confess I don't think much of it, but it may do." I was inclined to agree with him about the music, but after all was a little disappointed, because I had grown quite warm and interested in writing the words. They were on a subject that was then very near the hearts of the loyal people of the North [i.e. the fate of Northern prisoners of war in Confederate jails]. . . .

He concludes the account with the modest comment: "My successes were usually surprises."

Vive la Compagnie

According to James Fuld's excellent reportage in *The Book of World-Famous Music*, no early printing of this song has been found in France though it would seem to be of French origin. Prototypes have been found in nineteenth-century German song collections, and it is quite reminiscent of the English tune known as "Lincolnshire Poacher."

"Vive la Compagnie" made its way to the U.S. some time before 1844, when it was published by F. D. Benteen of Baltimore, one of Stephen Foster's early publishers. This early American version of the song is virtually the same as is known in the twentieth century. It is of course a drinking song, and the Benteen title page informs us that it was "Sung by the Maryland Cadet's [*sic*] Glee Club." Since drinking and drinking songs seem eternally popular with both glee clubs and cadets, it remained a great favorite with those groups for a hundred years or more.

Wait for the Wagon

Of the many different editions of this charming and immensely popular piece that appeared in the U.S. and abroad beginning at mid-century, a copy of the first known printing is reproduced here. It was published in 1851 by F. D. Benteen of Baltimore. The first edition credits the piece to one George P. Knauff, but if this is the case Knauff's contemporaries apparently ignored him while making his song famous: his name is not mentioned in any standard reference book dealing with popular music. Of course, one should really say that the Benteen edition *implies* that this Knauff was composer: the title page identifies "Wait for the Wagon" as an "Ethiopian [i.e. minstrel] Song *for the Piano Forte* by Geo. P. Knauff" (italics added). This could mean that Knauff simply made up a piano accompaniment for an existing tune and text and wrote it all out for this edition; that he was, in other words, a musical arranger for Benteen. Nineteenth-century publishers did not always wish to spell out exactly who composed a song or who was merely an arranger. Sometimes the publisher did not even *know* who composed a certain song.

In his *Songs That Never Die* (1894), the writer Henry F. Reddall stated that "Wait for the Wagon" was by R. Bishop Buckley (1810–1867), an Englishman who settled in the U.S. and organized a minstrel troupe in the 1840s. One early edition of the song did present it "as sung by Buckley's Minstrels." Other editions of the 1850s—those of Oliver Ditson, for instance—seem to credit the piece to "GAS," whoever or whatever that meant. Certainly, the actual author of the delightful song should have had no cause to deny it; even if melodically repetitious, it has a distinctive warmth, color and energy.

We Won't Go Home Till Morning

This slight but tenacious bit of melody, and the string of different texts associated with it, have inspired a rather amazing historical coverage in several languages. One can read about it in such diverse sources as the *Journal of American Folklore*, *Canciones Musical Popular Español*, the *Zeitschrift für Musikwissenschaft* and *Grove's Dictionary of Music and Musicians*. A vintage New York periodical, *The*

Opera Magazine, ran an article entitled "What Is the World's Most Famous Song" and answered its own question resoundingly:

> There cannot be the slightest question that ["We Won't Go Home Till Morning"] is the song which is the best known and most widely sung throughout the whole world in this year of grace 1915.

Most of the song's pedigrees are apocryphal—that it was an ancient Spanish or Arabic melody, that it was brought to Europe by Crusaders who had heard it in Jerusalem, that it was inspired by the death of the Duke of Marlborough. One of the most charming anecdotes about the song, however, turns out to be documented fact: around 1781 it was sung at Versailles by a nursemaid, a country girl, to one of the children of Marie Antoinette and Louis XVI; *Grove's* says that Antoinette was "immensely taken with the song, and presently all the court were singing it." The text that they sang began "Malbrouk s'en va-t-en guerre":

> Malbrouk is going to war,
> Mironton, ton ton mirontaine,
> Malbrouk is going to war,
> And doesn't know when he'll return.

This led to general popularity and wide publication of the song during the 1780s in France, England and elsewhere. The text beginning "We Won't Go Home Till Morning" was a nineteenth-century English invention and was first published in both England and America in the 1840s (the William Clifton arrangement reproduced here was copyrighted in 1842). "For He's a Jolly Good Fellow," certainly the text that became the best known and most used, was apparently also invented by the English sometime later in the century. It was published in America in the 1905 collection *Folk Songs of Many Nations*, edited by Louis C. Elson, who classed it as an English folksong and called it "the carol of the modern rollicker."

This tune was also quoted prominently by Ludwig van Beethoven. He used it to represent French troops in his *Wellington's Victory, or The Battle of Vittoria*, Opus 91 (in the score Beethoven marked the tune "Marcia: Marlborough"), which he composed in 1813, just 32 years after that nurse sang the tune to the child of Marie Antoinette.

When I Saw Sweet Nelly Home

The cover of the 1859 Pond edition reprinted here bears a signed statement by the composer, John Fletcher: "An unauthorized and incorrect copy of this song has been published under my name but without my consent. This is the ONLY CORRECT EDITION." Fletcher was apparently referring to the first edition of the song published by William Paine in Portland, Maine, with the notice of an 1856 copyright registered by J. S. Paine (William's brother). One of the 1856 issues has an elaborately illustrated cover that provides a clue as to how the brothers Paine probably came to appropriate the song: it pictures the Perham Minstrel Troupe of New York in action and lists "Nelly" as one of the "Gems of the Perham's Minstrelsy."

If John Fletcher operated like some other songwriters of the day, including Stephen Foster early in his career, he gave out manuscript copies of his songs to minstrel performers with the hope that his work might get a public hearing. This practice frequently backfired when manuscripts fell into the hands of publishers and were issued with or without credit to the composer and usually without any remuneration. It may be conjectured that the Perham troupe performed the unpublished "Nelly" on tour in 1856 and that the Paines grabbed it for publication; the pirated edition at least gave credit to Fletcher and his lyricist Frances Kyle.

One other enterprising resident of New England saw possibilities in "Nelly": Patrick S. Gilmore, the famed bandmaster and composer of "When Johnny Comes Marching Home." He also apparently heard the Perham troupe in 1856 and appropriated the Kyle text (without crediting the author) for his own setting; it was published that year by Russell & Tolman of Boston with a cover notice that read: "As Sung by Perham's Opera Company." Thus the case of "Nelly" provides an excellent reflection of the terribly casual ethics that were so frequently typical of nineteenth-century music publishing in America. Furthermore, the various editions of the famous song illustrate the vagaries of that growing and lucrative industry. Witness this little catalogue of curious details:

(1) The most famous line in the song is that which ends the verse and the chorus: "From Aunt Dinah's quilting party I was seeing Nelly home." It appears in the first edition (Paine). The first "official" edition (Pond), however, changes "Aunt Dinah's quilting party" to "an august evening party." Now, the substitution is not only inexplicable, the appearance of the word "august" is preposterous. Surely the word "August" was intended but was waylaid by one of the industry's typically careless typesetters. (If Fletcher was bent on improving the text, he missed the opportunity to dispense with the ghastly image of the "pink-eyed pimpernell" as well as the indelicate "path Where the cattle love to roam"; no farm boy in his right mind would walk his girl home at night on a route so adversely aromatic and hazardous to shoes.) In the "second" authorized edition issued after the renewal of the

copyright (in 1882 by Fletcher and 1884 by Ditson), "Aunt Dinah" is mysteriously reinstated, the "august evening party" banished.

(2) In all editions examined (including one as late as 1908 by Century Music) the covers identify the song's heroine as Nellie; yet in the caption titles (just above the music) and throughout the text she is consistently referred to as Nelly.

(3) The 1856 pirated edition credits [Miss] Frances Kyle as author of the text. Fletcher's edition omits any author credit. The cover page of the 1884 edition credits [Mr.] Francis Kyle, while page one of the very same edition credits [Miss] Frances Kyle.

None of these details is perhaps important to those who would simply enjoy the song for itself; but to anyone interested in establishing a clear record of nineteenth-century American music publishing—even a record of the most popular songs—such contradictions can mean a major headache.

When Johnny Comes Marching Home

Patrick Sarsfield Gilmore (1829–1892) was an Irish-born cornetist who came to Massachuetts by way of Canada in the late 1840s and eventually established himself as the most famous bandmaster in the country prior to John Philip Sousa. He achieved his first fame about ten years after his arrival as conductor of the Boston Brigade Band, which he transformed into Gilmore's Grand Boston Band and presented in formal concerts in its home city and elsewhere. He went south to the Civil War in 1861 as bandmaster of the Twenty-fourth Massachusetts Regiment and in 1863 was placed in charge of all the army bands in Louisiana.

It was in New Orleans in 1864 that he organized his first "monster concert," a kind of giant musical happening characterized dryly by Frederick H. Martens, author of the Gilmore article in the *Dictionary of American Biography*, an "an aberration of musical good taste peculiar to the period." Perhaps Gilmore derived his inspiration from the example set by New Orleans' own Louis Moreau Gottschalk, who had staged such events in Havana in 1860 and 1861.

Gilmore later organized two other giant musical events in Boston: the National Peace Jubilee (1869), celebrating the coming of peace after the Civil War, and the International Peace Jubilee (1872), supposedly celebrating the end of the Franco-Prussian War. Each of these great conclaves lasted for several days and featured concerts by massed orchestras, bands and choruses numbering thousands of performers, supplemented with spectacular sound effects by church bells, cannons and anvils.

Though he produced a body of popular instrumental music and songs, Gilmore's activities as bandmaster and festival-organizer overshadowed his work as composer. In this capacity he is remembered for one piece, the grand Civil War song "When Johnny Comes Marching Home" (1863), issued under the pseudonym Louis Lambert. There is controversy, however, over Gilmore's authorship of the tune since it appeared in print with different texts and no composer credit before and after the publication of "When Johnny Comes Marching Home." Some commentators believe the tune to be of Irish (or other) folk origin, but this has not been proved. Martens suggests in his article that Gilmore set his text to a tune he "brought" from New Orleans.

Whatever the actual source of the tune, Gilmore's "Johnny" survives as one of the strongest and most unusual songs of the period. Its form is not that of the conventional verse section followed by a refrain; it is constructed as a series of statements by a solo voice with responses by a chorus, and the pattern of these statements and responses is slightly different in the last two verses than in the first two. Furthermore, the little instrumental section that serves as prelude and postlude—it is actually an eight-measure variation on the first three notes of the tune—is used as an interlude between the second and third verses; it ends on an "open" chord, omitting the third, which in this context seems like the echo of a military fanfare. Finally, "Johnny" is one of relatively few songs in a minor key to achieve and maintain wide popularity.

When You and I Were Young, Maggie

This song was among the early successes of the post-Civil War era, a time when music publishers were confronted with a great drop in sheet-music sales after the flourishing market for war songs was over. It was published by the composer himself, James Austin Butterfield (1837–1891), first in Indianapolis in 1866 and then in Chicago about a year later. Butterfield, an Englishman who came to America in 1856, based his activities largely in Chicago and made a reputation there as choral conductor, teacher of singing, and composer. Other than "Maggie," his one great popular hit, and numerous other songs, he wrote anthems, orchestral works and at least five operas. One of the latter works, *Belshazzar* (c. 1873), a Biblical spectacle in five acts, was widely performed both on the stage and as a concert piece and was published in two different editions. (An account of Butterfield's career may be found in W. S. B. Mathews' *A Hundred Years of Music in America*; see Bibliography).

The author of the text of "When You and I Were Young, Maggie" was George Washington Johnson (1839–1917), a Canadian writer and teacher. Butterfield set the poem after seeing it in a collection of the author's pieces entitled *Maple Leaves,* published in Canada in 1864. Johnson's "Maggie" brings to mind two later popular products cut from similar cloth: Cooper's "Sweet Genevieve" and Rexford's "Silver Threads Among the Gold." Like "Genevieve," "Maggie" is said to have been inspired by the poet's young wife who died shortly after marriage (except the real Maggie died after her poem was written and the real Genevieve died before). And like "Silver Threads," "Maggie" is a reminiscence of youth by an aging husband in whose eyes the wife remains unchanged by age: "But to me you're as fair as you were, Maggie, when you and I were young."

The success of "Maggie" inspired several "answer" songs, including "The Past We Can Never Recall, Jamie" (1868) by Joseph P. Webster (composer of "Lorena") and Butterfield's own "Maggie's Answer" (1868). Over a hundred years later, the American film director Peter Bogdanovich provided another kind of response to "Maggie" by using it as a symbol of an era and a social class in his 1974 film version of the Henry James novella *Daisy Miller.* Bogdanovich's choice of song was entirely appropriate, but his handling of it in the film was perhaps misjudged. In a key sequence he has Daisy sing the piece in a mocking, almost jazzy manner, but it is unlikely that a middle-class girl of the period would have done it this way, not even one as blasé and unconventional as James's Daisy Miller.

To twentieth-century ears, "Maggie" and its sentiments may seem as creaky as that creaking old mill in the song's first verse, but to auditors and performers in the modest parlors of the 1860s and '70s it was fresh and poignant. It should not be surprising that at a time when thousands of young men had been lost in the war and the mortality rate among women under thirty was high, a simple, graceful song about a happy couple grown old together was regarded with fondness and sentiment by a large segment of the public.

Whispering Hope

"Whispering Hope" (1868) was the third song in Septimus Winner's great trilogy of popular hits, the earlier two being "Listen to the Mocking Bird" (1854) and "Der Deitcher's Dog" (1864). It was issued as the work of Alice Hawthorne, his favorite pseudonym. Charles Claghorn, Winner's biographer (and grandson), solemnly declares that "Whispering Hope" is the composer's "most classical" piece. It is true that the piece does betray certain pretensions to class in the "poetic" language of its text, the little runs and trills of its accompaniment and the mildly expansive soprano part which encompasses the range of a twelfth.

Early in its career, Winner's lilting duet waltzed its way into church choir lofts and enjoyed a long life there. Indeed, in the last quarter of the twentieth century it can still be found in certain churches that place few theological demands upon their musical repertories. It can also be found in many gospel songbooks. This church domination of the song's history is curious in that its text contains nothing really "religious," certainly nothing at all doctrinal, and the music itself is a child of the Victorian ballroom. Presumably it was the concept of hope that was considered somehow exclusively Christian and that led the little waltz-duet down the aisle. It was not only welcomed in Protestant churches but also, perhaps surprisingly, in precincts usually somewhat sterner: Winner's diary entry for 18 November 1901 reads: "Went down to Catholic Church with Gib to hear them play *Whispering Hope,* etc., in evening." One wonders what musical company that "etc." provided. Perhaps it would have been Louis Moreau Gottschalk's "The Last Hope," that other secular Victorian nosegay that got taken up for church duty.

Woodman! Spare That Tree!

Some of the original printings of this song included a lengthy letter from the author, George Pope Morris (1802–1864), to the composer, Henry Russell (1812–1900), relating the story behind the poem. The letter, dated 1 February 1837, apparently accompanied the manuscript of the poem (which Morris refers to as "The Oak") when it was delivered to Russell. The story is that Morris was out driving with a friend who took him to see a tree planted by the friend's grandfather near his childhood home. They discover the present tenant about to chop down the tree for firewood, but are able to save it by paying him ten dollars. An informal contract guaranteeing the life of the tree is drawn up on the spot and witnessed by the tenant's daughter.

When Henry Russell wrote his autobiography *Cheer! Boys, Cheer!* 58 years later, he retold this story, but in his version it is Russell himself and George Morris who are out driving and Morris whose grandfather had planted the tree and who bargains for its life. Misstatement and overstatement are no strangers to the Russell autobiography. It is a charming and amusing document of the period, but much of it must be taken with a grain of salt. The flamboyant British entertainer-songwriter apparently remembered incidents in his life as he wished them to be. He claims, for instance, to have composed and published over eight hundred songs, though the actual figure is around two hundred. He looks back on his career as a kind of social mission and makes extravagant claims for his work: he could blithely state that "slavery was one of the evils I helped to abolish through the medium of some of my songs" (Russell, p. 12). He believed that various of his ballads had contributed to the growth of the labor movement, brought about reform in insane asylums and encouraged the settling of the West. If the old showman had lived a century later, he would undoubtedly have seen his "Woodman! Spare That Tree!" as an important contribution to ecological preservation.

"Woodman" has features characteristic of the typical Russell ballad: it is rather long; it has a prominent, somewhat fancy piano part (Russell was his own accompanist when he performed and is said to have been an excellent pianist); it has a modest but effective vocal part; and it deftly exploits melodramatic subject matter. Unlike other Russell ballads, however, it leaves us at the finish not really knowing how the story turns out. Russell reports in *Cheer! Boys, Cheer!* (pp. 192–3) that once while he was performing "Woodman" a man in the audience jumped up and "in a very excited voice, called, 'Was the tree spared, sir?' 'It was,' I said. 'Thank God for that,' he answered, with a sigh of relief."

The Yellow Rose of Texas

The popularity of the delightful "Yellow Rose" has been as great in the twentieth century as it was in the last half of the nineteenth. The first printing of the song was apparently in 1858 under the imprint of William A. Pond & Co., New York, and Charles H. Brown, Jackson, Tennessee. The composer is unknown except for the initials "J. K." The original text, which may surprise some modern fans of the song, suggests that "Yellow Rose" was a product of the minstrel stage, though it is not written in dialect. And like several other minstrel songs of the 1850s it was taken over for military purposes by soldiers in the Civil War. "Yellow Rose" became associated with General John B. Hood, commander of the Confederate Army's "Texas Brigade." In 1864 General Hood was defeated at Nashville and he was replaced by General Joseph E. Johnson (nicknamed Uncle Joe). On the long retreat south, Hood's men sang a parody of "Yellow Rose" that made the song more famous than ever:

And now I'm going southward,
For my heart is full of woe;
I'm going back to Georgia
To find my Uncle Joe.
You may talk about your Beauregard
And sing of General Lee,
But the gallant Hood of Texas
Played hell in Tennessee.

The musical setting in the early editions of "Yellow Rose" has snappy syncopations and little rhythmic subtleties which unfortunately got lost as the song left the printed page and passed into oral tradition.

Zip Coon

This popular song of the early 1830s, which subsequently became known under the familiar title "Turkey in the Straw," was one of the earliest pieces used by individual blackface performers before the organization of minstrel troupes. The edition reprinted here (published between 1830 and 1835) features an extraordinary lithograph of the Zip Coon figure that was to become one of the leading prototypes of the minstrel show's stock cast of characters. He was the great dandy of the big cities, as opposed to the other early prototypical character, Jim Crow, who personified the simple plantation field hand. The lithograph (by Endicott of New York) presents in detail the essential features of the character: the expression of hauteur on the face, the carefully curled hair, the elaborate collar and jabot with stickpin, the eyeglasses on a long chain, the watch fob and ornamental jewlery dangling at the waist and—most important—the long swallow-tail jacket, which was always blue. (Another song of the 1830s celebrating the Zip Coon-type character was entitled "My Long Tail Blue.")

It is not known who originated "Zip Coon," though three early blackface performers claimed authorship: George Washington Dixon, who is mentioned on the cover of the edition used here; George Nichols, a pioneer blackface clown in circuses; and Bob Farrell, who was actually known as "Zip Coon" (he performed the song in New York in 1834). "Zip" was always danced as well as sung; the usual choreography is described by Carl Wittke in his excellent book *Tambo and Bones* (see Bibliography) as resembling " a rough jig dance . . . said to have originated among the boatmen, gamblers, quently for a real 'hoe-down' at a rendezvous near Natchez" (Wittke, p. 17).

Bibliography

This is not a general bibliography of the subject, but represents only that material actually used in preparing the Introduction and Commentary.

Benét, William Rose. *The Reader's Encyclopedia.* 2nd ed. New York, Thomas Y. Crowell, 1965.

Bland, James A. *The James A. Bland Album of Outstanding Songs.* Compiled, edited and arranged by Charles Haywood. New York, Edward B. Marks, 1946.

Brink, Carol. *Harps in the Wind. The Story of the Singing Hutchinsons.* New York, Macmillan, 1947.

British Minstrelsie. A representative collection of the songs of the nations . . . with articles, notes, and illustrations. 4 vols. Edinburgh, T. C. & E. C. Jack, 1895–96.

Chase, Gilbert. *America's Music.* Rev. 2nd ed. New York, McGraw-Hill, 1966.

Chosen Songs of the Civil War. Oklahoma City, Oklahoma Historical Society, 1960.

Claghorn, Charles Eugene. *Biographical Dictionary of American Music.* West Nyack, N.Y., Parker Publishing Co., 1973.

———. *The Mocking Bird; The Life and Diary of Its Author, Sep. Winner.* Philadelphia, The Magee Press, 1937.

Daly, John Jay. *A Song in His Heart.* [A biography of James A. Bland.] Philadelphia, The John C. Winston Co., 1951.

Dictionary of American Biography. New York, Charles Scribner's Sons, 1927.

Dressler, Louis R. *Favorite Masterpieces.* Vol. 1. New York and Chicago, The Standard Musical Association, 1897.

Dwyer, Richard A., and Richard E. Lingenfelter. *The Songs of the Gold Rush.* Berkeley and Los Angeles, University of California Press, 1964.

Elson, Louis C. *Folk Songs of Many Nations.* Cincinnati, The John Church Co., 1905.

Emurian, Ernest K. *The Sweetheart of the Civil War. The True Story of the Song "Lorena."* Natick, Mass., W. A. Wilde Co., 1962.

Epstein, Dena J. *Music Publishing in Chicago Before 1871: The Firm of Root & Cady, 1858–1871.* Detroit, Information Coordinators, Inc., 1969.

Fitz-Gerald, S. J. Adair. *Stories of Famous Songs.* London, John C. Nimmo, 1898.

Fuld, James J. *The Book of World-Famous Music.* Rev. & enl. ed. New York, Crown Publishers, Inc., 1971.

Geller, James J. *Famous Songs and Their Stories.* New York, The Macauley Company, 1931.

Grove's Dictionary of Music and Musicians. 5th ed. Edited by Eric Blom. New York, St. Martin's Press. Inc., 1954.

Haddon, Archibald. *The Story of the Music Hall; From Cave of Harmony to Cabaret.* London, Fleetway Press, 1935.

Hart, James D. *The Oxford Companion to American Literature.* 4th ed. New York, Oxford University Press, 1965.

Harwell, Richard B. *Confederate Music.* Chapel Hill, The University of North Carolina Press, 1950.

Hewitt, John Hill. *Shadows on the Wall.* Baltimore, Turnbull Brothers, 1877.

Hills, William H. *Students' Songs.* Boston, Rand Avery Co., 1887.

Hitchcock, H. Wiley. *Music in the United States: A Historical Introduction.* 2nd ed. Englewood Cliffs, N.J., Prentice-Hall, 1974.

Howard, John Tasker. *Our American Music; A Comprehensive History from 1620 to the Present.* 4th ed. New York, Thomas Y. Crowell, 1965.

Hudgins, Mary D. "Arkansas Traveler—A Multi-Parented Wayfarer." *Arkansas Historical Quarterly,* Vol. 30 (Summer 1971).

Huggins, Coy E. *John Hill Hewitt: Bard of the Confederacy.* [Dissertation, Florida State University.] Ann Arbor, Mich., University Microfilms, 1964.

Hughes, Josephine L., and Richard J. Wolfe. "The Tunes of 'The Bucket.'" *Bulletin of The New York Public Library,* Vol. 65, no. 9 (November 1961).

Hunt, William Southworth. "The Story of a Song." *Proceedings of the New Jersey Historical Society, 1933.* Newark, The New Jersey Historical Society, 1933.

The Hymnal 1940 Companion. New York, The Church Pension Fund, 1949.

Jackson, Richard. *United States Music: Sources of Bibliography and Collective Biography.* Brooklyn, Brooklyn College of the City University of New York, Institute for Studies in American Music, 1973.

Johnson, Helen Kendrick. *Our Familiar Songs and Those Who Made Them.* New York, Henry Holt and Co., 1881.

Kerr, Phil. *Music in Evangelism and Stories of Famous Christian Songs.* Rev. ed. Glendale, Calif., Gospel Music Publishers, 1944.

Lair, John. *Songs Lincoln Loved.* New York, Duell, Sloan and Pearce, 1954.

Lansingburgh, New York 1771–1971. Pamphlet prepared under the direction of Jane S. Lord. Lansingburgh, The Lansingburgh Historical Society, 1971.

Leisy, James F. *The Folk Song Abecedary.* New York, Hawthorn Books, Inc., 1966.

Loper, Samuel Ward. *The Life of Henry Clay Work . . .* written for the Middlesex County [Connecticut] Historical Society. [n.p., 1907?] [Reproduction of an unpublished typescript; Music Division, The New York Public Library.]

Lovering, Frank W. "Jingle Bells: Its Author Was a Rover." *Musical Courier*, Vol. 160, no. 6 (December 1959).

Macmillan, Ernest. *A Book of Songs.* New York, Dutton, 1929.

Macqueen-Pope, W. *The Melodies Linger On. The Story of Music Hall.* London, W. H. Allen, 1950.

Marcus, Geoffrey. *The Maiden Voyage.* New York, The Viking Press, 1969.

Mathews, W. S. B. *A Hundred Years of Music in America.* Chicago, G. L. Howe, 1889 (reprinted by AMS Press).

Miller, Kelly. "The Negro 'Stephen Foster;' The First Published Biography of James A. Bland." *The Etude*, Vol. 57, no. 7 (July 1939).

Nathan, Hans. *Dan Emmett and the Rise of Early Negro Minstrelsy.* Norman, University of Oklahoma Press, 1962.

Ninde, Edward S. *The Story of the American Hymn.* New York, The Abingdon Press, 1921.

Pulling, Christopher. *They Were Singing; And What They Sang About.* London, George G. Harrap & Co. Ltd, 1952.

Reddall, Henry Frederick. *Songs That Never Die.* Washington, D.C., J. R. Jones, 1894.

Root, George F. *The Story of a Musical Life.* Cincinnati, The John Church Co.; Chicago, Root & Sons, 1891.

Russell, Henry. *Cheer! Boys, Cheer! Memories of Men and Music.* London, John Macqueen, 1895.

Sankey, Ira D. *Sankey's Story of the Gospel Hymns.* Philadelphia, The Sunday School Times Co., 1906.

Silber, Irwin. *Songs of the Civil War.* New York, Columbia University Press, 1960.

———. *Songs of the Great American West.* New York, The Macmillan Co., 1967.

Simpson, Harold. *A Century of Ballads, 1810–1910.* London, Mills & Brown, 1910.

Staton, Kate E. *Old Southern Songs of the Period of the Confederacy.* New York, Samuel French, 1926.

Turner, Michael R. *The Parlour Song Book.* London, Michael Joseph, 1972.

"What Is the World's Most Famous Song." *The Opera Magazine* (May 1915).

Wittke, Carl. *Tambo and Bones; A History of the American Minstrel Stage.* Durham, N.C., Duke University Press, 1930.